The

LYRIC GENIUS

of

CATULLUS

By E. A. HAVELOCK

Sometime Scholar of Emmanuel College, Cambridge
Sterling Professor of Classics, Yale University

NEW YORK / RUSSELL & RUSSELL

OTHER BOOKS by ERIC A. HAVELOCK

THE CRUCIFIXION OF INTELLECTUAL MAN

THE LIBERAL TEMPER in GREEK POLITICS

PREFACE to PLATO

FIRST PUBLISHED IN 1939

REISSUED, 1967, BY RUSSELL & RUSSELL

A DIVISION OF ATHENEUM PUBLISHERS, INC.

BY ARRANGEMENT WITH ERIC A. HAVELOCK

L. C. CATALOG CARD NO: 67-15472

ISBN: 0-8462-0967-5

PRINTED IN THE UNITED STATES OF AMERICA

Here is the record writ
  In every part,
Here the passion of it
  And here the smart;
Here the quick happiness
  Of love's first pride,
And here the last distress
  Of love denied.

Here is folly and flame,
  Canker and rust,
Railing and bitter blame,
  Ashes and dust.
Labour too soon betrayed
  By death's defeat.
But the Muse in time had made
  The work complete.

PREFACE TO THE SECOND PRINTING

THIS BOOK, if memory serves, may first have appeared on the booksellers' shelves about the day when Hitler invaded Poland. It is possible now to recall, but not recapture, the mood in which such a study had then seemed useful and even challenging. Up to that time, it would be true to say that Catullus had not received the amount of attention, from scholars and translators, which has since placed him near the center of Latin studies. Those were the days when the Muse often chose to consort with Karl Marx, and writers of varying allegiances kept in step with the causes that they served. It was difficult to view a poet so purely personal and private, so obviously non-ideological, as very important. Conversely, if one was interested enough in him to examine his poetic attitudes and technique, the examination was likely to turn into the argument that he was a very private poet.

This indeed is what happened. *The Lyric Genius of Catullus* became a defence of the proposition that experience so personal as to be ephemeral, born out of personal relationships which are equally ephemeral, furnishes occasion for a certain kind of poetry which is remembered with gratitude. The point does not need so much pressing today, and if in the last twenty years the work here reprinted has done something to alter the critical climate in which Catullus is being read and generally discussed, let that stand as its claim on present attention.

It appears indeed that the book has had an influence not foreseen when I wrote it. Only five hundred copies of the original edition were printed, and it did not seem likely that what it then had to say would make much impression in a world filled with the noise of war. Yet many have told me they have found the book a pleasant companion, and a serious one, and for their approval I am grateful. Since it has been so long out of print and therefore unable to correct by its actual statements many things that have been attributed to it, I have thought it worthwhile here to recapitulate what seem to me, as I arrange them in retrospect, the salient points of the critical estimate which it offers.

The first would be the stress laid on the presence in the poet's work—I refer to the entire Catullan corpus, not merely the selection here examined—of a special kind of emotional sincerity which is not allied to moral principle, or structured attitude, but is to be defined by its direct intensity and intimate application. Fierce loyalties and equally fierce disillusionments, erotic identification and also alienation, close affection and bitter contempt, vie with each other in these poems as the hallmarks of a personal exposure wholly devoid of hypocrisy.

But, secondly, this Catullan brand of sincerity is allied to what might seem to be its opposite, an urbanized sophistication, at once elegant and ironic, for which the preferred vehicle is the quick small talk of the salon or the street corner. No rustic enjoyment here of natural beauties, nor contemplation of the eternal verities, but something closer to a conversation, carried on by cultivated people who know how to use the nuances of allusion and the understatement of colloquialism. The Catullan irony is the connecting link which unites his sincerity and his sophistication. It does not undercut his emotional commitments, but places them in perspective.

If these be the quality of the poet's temper, the proof lies in his language. That is where to look for the evidence, and here in the third place I sought to elucidate the paradox of his genius by stressing the combination of sincerity with scholarship. I argued that the Alexandrianism, drawing upon the resources of history, mythology and literature, can add a romantic dimension to the poet's personal statement, and that his verbal artistry can manipulate various types of symmetry which are both acoustic and symbolic, and are at least as complex as those employed by the Elizabethans.

Fourth in my present order, though first in the original order of this book, comes the premise that it is the critic's first business to approach the poems autonomously, as completed statements, the significance of which lies in the statement, and in the structure employed to express it, without prior benefit of biographical or historical control.

It was these four critical propositions which then amalgamated themselves into the fifth, the central thesis of the book's title: Catullus is remembered with affection as a lyrist and he always will be. This is a fact of life, and it corresponds to a basic fact about his art. The peculiar virtues which are his and which are described above are not amenable to lengthy verbal extension. For such a poet, the kind of effort required to maintain a construct of considerable length is likely to dissipate his lyric energy without supplying an adequate substitute. Of the so-called longer poems, two are successful precisely because they are so breathless that the long poem becomes a long lyric. If the remainder afford discussion for scholars, as they always will, this is not because they are better, but because they are longer, so that there is quantitatively more in them to explore.

Of these five propositions, it is the third and fourth which seem, since I wrote, to have found most favor. This is understandable when we recall that estimates of Catullus made in the years before my own book appeared derived their color from the Romantics rather than from the poetry of Hopkins, Eliot and Pound, and were equally innocent of the New Criticism which, when applied to modern poetry in many tongues, has successfully established the doctrine that a poem deserves to be judged autonomously. But I would hazard the statement that in Catullus an alliance of learning and liberty, of sophistication and simplicity, of passion and irony, which I regard as peculiar to him, continues to evade even those who would view him in perspectives which seem modern.

Aside from the correction of a few errors and infelicities, the text of this reprint stands as it was first issued in 1939. It need not be assumed that the discussion here offered of the poet's intentions, because it is unaltered, is therefore to be regarded as definitive. On the contrary, one becomes aware, on rereading a composition that took shape under the same hand more than thirty years ago, of a sort of youthful alter ego, prepared to perform a task which in retrospect seems less than complete. There are important matters, dealing with the poet's Hellenistic inheritance and his Roman idiom, which are here indicated but not exhaustively explored. Critical comments are made at the expense of Vergil and Horace which today I would revise. Some sallies at the expense of classical learning scholars will find justly irritating. Let me confess that they now irritate me, even though they still seem not undeserved. A truly "revised" edition, which this is not, would have to take just account of that considerable amount of discriminating scholarship (including a new Oxford text) which in the years since this book first appeared has continued to recommend Catullus to the taste of English readers. Yet it has seemed best to reissue the work with its youthful integrity unimpaired, rather than attempt to tamper with a text which if expanded might have to be rewritten. And who shall say that the rewriting would be any better?

E . A . H .

New Milford, Connecticut
March, 1967

THE PREFACE

THIS book has been composed within narrow limitations, and makes none of the claims proper to a severe work of scholarship. In some sense it can be regarded as a by-product of lectures in which I have sought to interpret Catullus to several generations of undergraduates in this college. It owes an inevitable debt to Ellis and Munro, and in particular to Tenney Frank, whose work I gratefully acknowledge has inspired me even where, as occasionally, I have rejected the results of what I have called the biographical method of interpretation.

If apology is needed for a book which has been a labour of love rather than learning, I may plead that the discovery of the charms of Catullan lyric has been my diversion ever since my schooldays. Some of the responsibility for this must rest with W. H. Balgarnie, of Leys School, who as my formmaster once encouraged my early attempts at imitation. I believe, indeed, that the fourteenth version in this collection first appeared in the school magazine, though it has suffered much alteration since then.

I should like to express my thanks to Professor Gilbert Norwood, whose detailed criticisms have not only suggested many corrections and improvements in the text, but have helped to inspire its final shape and arrangement.

E. A. H.

Victoria College, Toronto, June, 1938

THE CONTENTS

PART THE FIRST
IMITATION of TWENTY-SIX LYRICS

CONTENTS

PART THE SECOND

ANALYSIS of the CATULLAN TEMPER

ERRATA

page 2, line 15: *for* Republican *read* republican

page 4, line 7: *for* 'little books *read* 'little books'

page 6, line 4: *for* Ebria acina *read* Ebrioso acino

page 39, line 4: *for* slibe *read* sible

page 61, fifth stanza, first line: *for* It is impossible *read* How hard it is

page 64, line 4: *for* at *read* et

page 66, line 29: *for* born *read* boon

page 66, line 31: *for* panuca *read* pauca

page 80, line 8: *for* 20 *read* 13

page 81, line 12: *for* proconsul for the province of Asia for that year, *read* propraetor for the province of Bithynia,

page 103, line 10: *for* pp. 30, 58.) *read* pp. 30, 58, 62.)

page 108, line 3: *for* funny *read* delightful

page 124, lines 13 and 14: *for* read them over, *read* scanned them,

page 126, line 28: *for* place *read* places

page 130, line 30: *for* grace *read* face

page 175, line 26: *for* marked *read* warned

page 175, line 27: *for* fail *read* would fail

page 179, line 9: *for* are *read* is

page 181, line 5: *for* sheep in skins go clad *read* graze the tender sheep

page 182, line 10: *for* work- *read* word-

page 185, note 5, line 5: *for* echnique *read* technique

page 187, lines 1 and 2: *for* territories recently conquered by Caesar *read* original Gallia Narbonensis,

page 188, note 46, line 1: *for* practical joker *read* man of humour

page 191, note 95, line 2: *for* simplified *read* condensed

page 192, note 102, line 2: *for* collecton *read* collection

INDEX

PART I

IMITATION OF TWENTY·SIX LYRICS

I. THE LANGUAGE OF LYRIC

ABOUT fifty years before the birth of Christ, Italy lost a poet who was still in his youth. Rome had known him well, but he was not her son, for he came from the district of Cisalpine Gaul to the north, which in those days, as we know from his own verse, was still known as 'the province.' Verona in the valley of the Po was his birthplace, but he must have lived a good deal of his life at Rome, besides spending a year abroad. At Rome he mixed in fashionable and literary society, found his friends and made some enemies among the leading writers and politicians of the age, and fell violently in love with a brilliant and distinguished woman whom in his verse he always called 'Lesbia.' She was almost certainly Clodia, wife of one Metellus, a prominent politician and proconsul, herself a member of the Gens Claudia, and therefore of the ruling caste of Republican Rome. To express his emotions both as friend and lover, the emotions of an educated and sensitive man, he turned to verse, and at once created for himself a unique place in ancient literature by writing the most passionate lyrics in the Latin tongue. Their utterance was soon stopped, for he died when he was about thirty, like a flame going out, so intense and youthful seems his genius. So died Keats of disease when he was twenty-six, and Burns of drink and poverty at thirty-seven, and Shelley, drowned at sea when he was thirty.

How shall one communicate to the English mind the essence of a Latin poet long dead ? He was once significant not as a historical figure but as a vehicle of intense emotion conveyed in rhythm and phrase. Therefore the story of his life and times, however cunningly uncovered, cannot recreate this spell. To translate his works constitutes an amusing but fatuous exercise of the wits; the translator, taxed to render meaning and construction, has no time to tune himself to the quick essential feeling which it was the poet's one business to express. And to enumerate his poetic virtues is like telling a friend how we enjoyed a certain joke, without telling him the joke.

This book in two short parts attempts the task of communication by methods which have a different emphasis. The twenty-six English verses which compose Part I are not 'translations' of Catullus as that word is usually understood, but rather imitations constructed to express a certain direct feeling which some of his verses have been able to communicate to me. They represent only a fraction of the whole, because, while the intellect can render translations to order, inspiration and feeling are wayward and incalculable. I may 'like' three-quarters of what Catullus wrote, but the impulse to give his mood its proper English shape is rare and accidental.

Yet this is not to say that the writing of my own verses has been uninstructed. Sympathy breeds an effort of analysis, and the effort in turn fresh sympathy. This wrestling with his poetry has revealed to me some things about it of a sort that professional scholars and critics are not usually interested to notice. Therefore in Part II I have added, as a sort of supplement to my rhymes, some account of my own discovery—naturally not complete—of the poet's style and substance. A poet's products have often been likened to jewels. The Catullan lyrics are rather flashes from a single stone of complex colours. Behind the metre and words lurks the Catullan temper, a subtle compound of wit and feeling, sophisticated yet direct, which has too often eluded even those who thought they knew him.

AT the head of the brief manuscript collection which comprises Catullus' memorial stands this short dedication, placed there probably by some editor's hand, since a poet who died in his early thirties is unlikely to have had time to muster his brief output in a single edition. More probably he issued his verses from time to time as he wrote them, in 'little books, each with its dedication. (Part II, note 3.) The present lines, slight though they are, carry the stamp of the man and his style:

> *Cui dono lepidum novum libellum*
> *Arida modo pumice expolitum?*
> *Corneli, tibi, namque tu solebas*
> *Meas esse aliquid putare nugas,*
> *Iam tum, cum ausus es unus Italorum*
> *Omne aevum tribus explicare chartis*
> *Doctis, Iuppiter, et laboriosis!*
> *Quare habe tibi quidquid hoc libelli*
> *Qualecunque ; quod, o patrona virgo,*
> *Plus uno maneat perenne saeclo.*

In this fashion he confesses allegiance to that new contemporary school of lyric (*nugae*), whose creed was fastidious elegance (*lepidum libellum*), a confession tempered with a self-depreciation which is touched with irony. Such are some of those characteristics of style and temper which are noticed in the Second Part. The reader for his amusement may also compare the epilogue (page 182) composed by Horace in a very different key for his own more pretentious odes.

To translate the second line of the verse is to discover the futility of translation, and the necessity of using more indirect methods to communicate poetic symbols from one language to another. Compare the essay on the *Impermanence of Poetry*, page 147, where the line is cited to illustrate this point.

DEDICATION TO CORNELIUS NEPOS,
HISTORIAN
OF CISALPINE GAUL

NOW has the printing-press
Crowned my ambition
By issuing this first
    Dainty edition!
Take it, Cornelius,
    Who liked them so—
My bits of verse—and that
    Was long ago,
When you had just begun
    What was to be
Your master work, the first
    World-history.
And wasn't it profound,
    Learned, and such!
Well, here's this book. I know
    It isn't much—
A bit of a thing. And yet
    O may it stay,
My lady Muse, awhile,
    Though men decay?

Minister vetuli puer Falerni,
Inger mi calices amariores,
Ut lex Postumiae iubet magistrae,
Ebria acina ebriosioris.
At vos quo libet hinc abite, lymphae,
Vini pernicies, et ad severos
Migrate: hic merus est Thyonianus.

IF his dedication was an intimate confession, these lines on the contrary are to be sung riotously with one foot on the table. Yet he has managed both moods in the same metre (the 'eleven-syllable'), and it will appear again as the vehicle of passionate address (Lesbia's Kisses, page 14) and morbid despair (Swan Song, page 68). No other poet of antiquity was skilful enough to discover in so tiny a metre such daring resources.

DRINKING SONG

BOY with the brimming beaker,
The banquet rules declare
The wine shall not grow weaker
  (A lady's in the chair).

List while her sovereign pleasure
  Decrees we drink it neat;
Then pour, O pour, a measure
  With alcohol replete.

Hence, hence, corroding water:
  Teetotallers console.
Bacchus you often slaughter,
  But here he's rescued whole!

> *Paene insularum, Sirmio, insularumque*
> *Ocelle, quascumque in liquentibus stagnis*
> *Marique vasto fert uterque Neptunus,*
> *Quam te libenter quamque laetus inviso,*
> *Vix mi ipse credens Thyniam atque Bithynos*
> *Liquisse campos et videre te in tuto.*
> *O quid solutis est beatius curis,*
> *Cum mens onus reponit, ac peregrino*
> *Labore fessi venimus larem ad nostrum*
> *Desideratoque adquiescimus lecto?*
> *Hoc est quod unum est pro laboribus tantis.*
> *Salve, o venusta Sirmio, atque ero gaude.*
> *Gaudete vosque, o Lydiae lacus undae.*
> *Ridete, quidquid est domi cachinnorum.*

THIS is written in iambics, but with a sort of slight stagger at the end of the line ('limping iambics')—a metre traditionally reserved for lampoons and trivialities. Here it becomes the instrument of sheer lyric—a striking example of how poetic genius may consist in pouring new wine into old bottles. However, the piece retains the occasional touch of ironical humour (for example, the double status of Sirmio, and the duplication of Neptune in order to have fresh water represented) and fantasy (as in the last line). His emotions in fact are sincere and yet sophisticated. The piece is analysed a little in Part II, both as a problem of translation and as a symptom of the Catullan temper (pages 97, 152). The one other specimen of limping iambic in this collection affords a striking contrast: it is the tragic soliloquy on page 52.

SALUTE TO SIRMIO

CHILD of the woods and waters,
How secretly you smile,
All ocean's isles excelling—
Yourself not quite an isle!
The Neptune brothers never
Could duplicate the charm
That greets my eye returning,
And makes my heart grow warm.

And have I really left them—
Far hill and dusty plain?
And do I now before you
Stand safe and sound again?
To reach home travel-weary
Our own fireside to greet,
And slacken off the burden—
Is anything so sweet?

To sink upon the pillow
We loved in distant dreams
Is the one compensation
For toil that heavy seems.
Hail, Sirmio the lovely,
Garda, rejoice! I've come.
Laugh, rocks and waves, laugh loudly:
The master is come home.

OF the remaining twenty-three verses in this collection, all but two tell the story of his love for Lesbia. They follow the order of their moods, from devoted rapture through doubt and disillusionment to inner conflict and despair. This may assist the reader to follow the poet's emotional journey with due order and propriety, but we may be sure that it was not so easy to follow in life. What irrational extremes of happiness and despair may have intervened between his first meeting with her and the day when he thought he had cast her off can be imagined only by those who have themselves loved extravagantly and unhappily.

Though it was 'Lesbia' who thus left such an enduring print on his most powerful poetry, we shall never know what she looked like herself. His verse has not allowed her face, hands and hair to be rescued from their dust. In one passage her flesh and blood momentarily appear 'moving on whispering feet,' till he sees her standing poised in the doorway, 'divinely fair.' In one other verse we catch the tinkle of her laugh—*dulce ridentem*, a simple phrase, itself a reminiscence of Sappho, which Horace afterwards remembered. Elsewhere, we hear only of her Lesbian name, and her ways —her gaiety, her agile wit, her distracting charm—'making fun so adorably when the mood takes her' (*cum . . . carum nescio quid libet iocari*, p. 18), and again 'making vows to high heaven, so pretty, so amusing, and so naughty of her' (*Et hoc pessima se puella vidit iocose lepide vovere divis*, No. 36).

These are only flashes. The record generally is of his own absorbing emotions, which he has mirrored so faithfully as to leave the impression of creating her portrait too. But this is an illusion. We do not see her, but only feel her as a power over him, for love and hate and anger and grief.

Ille mi par esse deo videtur,
Ille, si fas est, superare divos,
Qui sedens adversus identidem te
    Spectat et audit

Dulce ridentem, misero quod omnis
Eripit sensus mihi. Nam simul te,
Lesbia, aspexi, nihil est super mi
    Vocis in ore.

Lingua sed torpet, tenuis sub artus
Flamma demanat, sonitu suopte
Tintinant aures, gemina teguntur
    Lumina nocte . . .

Otium, Catulle, tibi molestum est ;
Otio exultas nimiumque gestis;
Otium reges prius et beatas
    Perdidit urbes.

THESE stanzas are an imitation of an ode of Sappho. Thus they not only adore his beloved, but are touched with the slight solemnity of historical reminiscence. In announcing his love, to himself if not to her, he chooses to gild it with the archaic glamour of a Greek poetess, dead these six hundred years, and now for the first time rendered by him into the Roman tongue. And when quick revulsion of feeling comes over him in the conclusion, it again serves to recall to him the melancholy romance of opulent and perished civilizations—which I have tried to imitate in 'Babylon.'

Thus, while Sappho's original was hungry, possessive and jealous, this Latin imitation is composed in a very different key (compare the discussions of it in Part II, pages 145, 149). Whether its two moods were part of the poet's own plan, or whether the last morbid stanza was fitted into this place by some later editor's hand, we shall never know.

BID ME TO LIVE

TO sit where I can see your face
And hear your laughter come and go
Is greater bliss than all the gods
      Can ever know.

The bright dream carries me away:
Watching your lips, your hair, your cheek,
I have so many things to say,
      Yet cannot speak.

I look, I listen, and my soul
Flames with a fire unfelt before
Till sense swims, and I feel and see
      And hear no more . . .

How rank this ease of lotus land:
I feel death in its dreamy spell.
The dreaming towers of Babylon—
      How soon they fell.

Vivamus, mea Lesbia, atque amemus,
Rumoresque senum severiorum
Omnes unius aestimemus assis.
Soles occidere et redire possunt:
Nobis, cum semel occidit brevis lux,
Nox est perpetua una dormienda.
Da mi basia mille, deinde centum,
Dein mille altera, dein secunda centum,
Deinde usque altera mille, deinde centum,
Dein, cum milia multa fecerimus,
Conturbabimus illa, ne sciamus,
Aut ne quis malus invidere possit,
Cum tantum sciat esse basiorum.

LESBIA'S KISSES

MY darling, let us live
  And love for ever.
They with no love to give,
  Who feel no fever,
Who have no tale to tell
  But one of warning—
The pack of them might sell
  For half a farthing.

The sunset's dying ray
  Has its returning,
But fires of our brief day
  Shall end their burning
In night where joy and pain
  Are past recalling—
So kiss me, kiss again—
  The night is falling.

Kiss me and kiss again,
  Nor spare thy kisses.
Let thousand kisses rain
  A thousand blisses.
Then, when ten thousand more
  Their strength have wasted,
Let's wipe out all the score
  Of what we've tasted:

Lest we should count our bliss
  To our undoing,
Or others grudge the kiss
  On kiss accruing.

Quaeris, quot mihi basiationes
Tuae, Lesbia, sint satis superque?
Quam magnus numerus Libyssae harenae
Laserpiciferis iacet Cyrenis,
Oraclum Iovis inter aestuosi
Et Batti veteris sacrum sepulcrum;
Aut quam sidera multa, cum tacet nox,
Furtivos hominum vident amores—
Tam te basia multa basiare
Vesano satis et super Catullo est,
Quae nec pernumerare curiosi
Possint nec mala fascinare lingua.

THIS little lyric is composed in language of a passionate simplicity, asking for kisses as uncountable as the sand or the stars. Why then complicate his comparison with mythology, and arrest the flow by inserting the three lines about Cyrene and Battus? Has the pedantry of Alexandrian scholarship for once overcome his song? My English version seeks to place a more favourable interpretation upon the lines: he has tinged the emotion of love with a feeling for historical romance, even as he did in the Sappho poem (page 12). Compare the essay in Part II on *The Romantic Scholar* (page 124).

LESBIA'S QUESTION

AND do you ask me this—
What is the ration
Of kisses you must kiss
    To quench my passion?
Africa's desert land
    Is wide, they say:
Think of the desert sand
    Of Africa.

On shrines of Egypt beat
    Suns without pity.
White is Cyrene's street,
    That storied city.
Between, the sands roll on;
    Their count is missing:
So bid the count begone
    When you are kissing.

The stars that make the sky
    Their nightly dwelling,
Twinkling while lovers sigh,
    But never telling:
Count these if you would find
    How often given
Your kiss could cure a mind
    By hunger riven.

Then could no malice tell
    What was the measure,
Nor tongue cast dreary spell
    Over our treasure.

THIS verse forms a study in a single sentence, a *tour de force* effective when the Latin inflections can tie the words together, but scarcely possible in English. It provides an apt illustration (page 149) of the technical problems which arise when an inflected language has to be paraphrased in one which is not inflected:

> *Passer, deliciae meae puellae,*
> *Quicum ludere, quem in sinu tenere,*
> *Cui primum digitum dare adpetenti*
> *Et acris solet incitare morsus,*
> *Cum desiderio meo nitenti*
> *Carum nescio quid libet iocari*
> *(Ut solaciolum sui doloris,*
> *Credo, ut tum gravis adquiescat ardor)—*
> *Tecum ludere sicut ipsa possem*
> *Et tristis animi levare curas!*

Though in form an address to the 'sparrow' (page 147), the vocative is left suspended, as it can be in Latin, and the subject of the poem becomes the bird's mistress rather than the bird itself. My own imitation pursues the same effect, but more directly, as the idiom of English requires. Compare also the conclusion of the next piece, where a lament on the bird's death finds its climax in the thought that it has brought a tear to Lesbia's eye!

WHEN LESBIA PLAYS

ON you, her singing bird,
   Her kisses fall,
Held ever at her breast,
   Loved more than all.
Her hand hovers all day
   To catch and miss
And catch again a quick
   Canary's kiss.

What thing is merrier,
   What sight is softer,
Than that bright head adored
   Bending in laughter?
So can keen merriment
   Stifle the sigh
That love puts in her heart—
   Ah, would that I

Could rest my aching love
   As she can do,
Sharing, canary bird,
   The ache with you.

THIS, as I have sought to show (page 111), is for all its prettiness an ironic little piece, and impassioned attempts to turn
it into sonnet form do it both more and less than justice:

> *Lugete, o Veneres Cupidinesque*
> *Et quantum est hominum venustiorum!*
> *Passer mortuus est meae puellae,*
> *Passer, deliciae meae puellae,*
> *Quem plus illa oculis suis amabat ;*
> *Nam mellitus erat, suamque norat*
> *Ipsam tam bene quam puella matrem,*
> *Nec sese a gremio illius movebat,*
> *Sed circumsiliens modo huc modo illuc*
> *Ad solam dominam usque pipiabat.*
> *Qui nunc it per iter tenebricosum*
> *Illuc unde negant redire quemquam.*
> *At vobis male sit, malae tenebrae*
> *Orci, quae omnia bella devoratis:*
> *Tam bellum mihi passerem abstulistis.*
> *Vae factum male! Vae miselle passer!*
> *Tua nunc opera meae puellae*
> *Flendo turgiduli rubent ocelli.*

The lines reflect that urban, sophisticated idiom which
composed such an important ingredient in the Catullan temper (Part II, pages 102, 111). The conclusion reveals that this,
like the previous piece, is a love-poem in disguise. The bird's
death provides a charming excuse for lamenting the tear in
Lesbia's eye.

LESBIA'S TEARS

GRACES and Cupid choirs,
   Bow every head.
True lovers tune your lyres:
   Dirge for the dead.
My lady's little bird—
   Her darling one
More than her eyes preferred—
   Is dead and gone.

The tiny thing beguiled
   Her heart all day,
Charming her as a child
   Its mother may,
Hopping from room to room,
   Piping its song.
Now—what a road of gloom
   It hops along!

Must prettiness still feel
   Death's fatal sting?
Then cursed be death, to steal
   Her pretty thing.
To see her eyes all blurred
   And hear her cry
How can I bear? O bird
   Why did you die?

THOUGH he never tells us what his own Lesbia looked like, he can itemize the charms of her rivals with cruel gusto, as in the two succeeding verses. His first victim, we may infer from other and unprintable verses, was one Ameana from Gaul, mistress of Julius Caesar's lieutenant and chief engineer Mamurra, the *decoctor*.

> *Salve, nec minimo puella naso,*
> *Nec bello pede nec nigris ocellis,*
> *Nec longis digitis nec ore sicco,*
> *Nec sane nimis elegante lingua,*
> *Decoctoris amica Formiani.*
> *Ten provincia narrat esse bellam?*
> *Tecum Lesbia nostra comparatur?*
> *O saeclum insapiens et infacetum!*

LESBIA'S RIVALS (I)

O LIPS and Nose and Hands and Feet,
Not very small or very neat:
O Eyes all languishing, that seen
More close, grow evidently green:
O Mouth extended far and wide,
Home of the Tongue that wags inside—
To charm continue, if you can,
That bankrupt bum you call a man.
Out in the provinces, I hear,
They match you with my own dear fair.
Match you! Good Lord! Are men all mad
To show taste so completely bad?

Quintia formosa est multis, mihi candida, longa,
  Recta est. Haec ego sic singula confiteor,
Totum illud 'formosa' nego. Nam nulla venustas,
  Nulla in tam magno est corpore mica salis.
Lesbia formosa est, quae cum pulcherrima tota est,
  Tum omnibus una omnes subripuit Veneres.

ON the importance of *sal* and *venustas* see Part II, pages
105, 120.

LESBIA'S RIVALS (II)

THEY tell me Quintia's a beauty.
 It's true she's fair and straight and tall.
Such qualities, considered singly,
 Will help her case. She needs them all.
But how can beauty be allowed her?
 O breast and thigh and arm so round,
O lump magnificent, what flavour
 Of fascination have you found?

To Lesbia turn for beauty's pattern.
 There every part is fair and glad.
What's more, she's stolen all the graces
 That all her rivals might have had.

Nulla potest mulier tantum se dicere amatam
  Vere, quantum a me Lesbia amata mea es.
Nulla fides ullo fuit unquam in foedere tanta
  Quanta in amore tuo ex parte reperta mea est.

THESE four lines with their balanced mathematical structure (page 139) provide a perfect specimen of that ancient
verse-form known technically as the epigram. Six of the
species here come together in this collection, of which this
is the second. All of them are written in elegiac couplets.
Exactly what the term epigram may mean is discussed in
Part II, pages 135–137. These six specimens reveal how his
powerful genius could manipulate the elegiac couplet as
successfully as the lighter metres, to cover a wide variety of
emotion. The first and third are gay and frivolous; the second
and fourth passionate, the last two solemn and sorrowful.
Later on in this collection occur six more of equal variety
and intensity.

MY TRUE LOVE HATH MY HEART

THERE never was a woman who could say,
            And say it true,
That she was loved of any, O my love,
            As I love you.
There never was a loyal promise given
            Faithful and free,
As loyalty to you, because I love you,
            Is given from me.

Lesbia mi dicit semper male nec tacet unquam
De me: Lesbia me dispeream nisi amat.
Quo signo? quia sunt totidem mea: deprecor illam
Adsidue, verum dispeream nisi amo.

THE flexibility of this dactylic metre, the variety of effects he can produce with it in different poems, and consequently the freedom with which I have varied the form of my own imitations, are explained on page 157.

AMANTIUM IRAE

AH, my love, her lips how pretty!
       And how cruel!
Angry with me, to her anger
       Adding fuel.
Yet she loves me, and I know it:
       Here's the sign:
My tongue's as sharp, yet no heart loves her
       More than mine!

THE original Latin of this, if the truth be told, is not all poetry:

> *Si cui quid cupido optantique obtigit unquam*
> *Insperanti, hoc est gratum animo proprie.*
> *Quare hoc est gratum nobis quoque, carius auro,*
> *Quod te restituis, Lesbia, mi cupido.*
> *Restituis cupido atque insperanti, ipsa refers te*
> *Nobis. O lucem candidiore nota!*
> *Quis me uno vivit felicior, aut magis hac res*
> *Optandas vita dicere quis poterit?*

The first half of the verse is an attempt at epigram construction, but this time the effect is clumsy:

    cupido . . . optanti . . . insperanti   in lines 1, 2 balance
    cupido . . . cupido . . . insperanti   in lines 4, 5;
    gratum . . . in line 2 balances *gratum . . .* in line 3;

and in general the thought of lines 1 and 2 is balanced by the fact of lines 3 and 4.

The attempt fails, I think, because he is striving after another effect at the same time, namely, the expression of intense emotion in unemotional terms, reduced to the language of bare prose, of the sort which he uses successfully in the famous *Odi et Amo* (below, page 58). This bare prose-poetry style of his, which he rarely attempts, is the nearest he comes to Wordsworthian 'plainness of diction,' and is quite different from the artless half-colloquial manner which he employs in his sophisticated lyrics.

In the last half of the verse he abandons the attempt at epigram and reverts to sheer lyric.

REUNION

TO dream of something dear, in hopeless yearning,
And find the dream come true, is joy complete.
Dear love, I dreamt of you and your returning,
    Dreams sad and sweet.

To-day you have come back, and sorrow's over.
    I never thought, seeing you go away,
Joy could so fill the heart of any lover
    As mine this day.

III. LOVE AND DEATH

'THE night is falling,' he had told Lesbia when he was pleading for her kisses. In the two following poems he turns from love to look on the grave. The first of them might be described as a short elegy (compare page 140) on the death of his brother. The second tries to console a close friend who had lost his wife. The loss of his brother seems to have cast a slightly morbid shadow over the rest of his life; he recalls it more than once elsewhere with a reiterated and passionate bitterness (page 116), and in this elegy, facing his own bereavement, he accepts death as the final defeat of affection. For his friend's benefit, however, he can in the next epigram draw some consolation from the thought that perhaps the grave hears us; but his words lack that confident ring which belongs only to the ages of faith.

It is not inappropriate to place these two verses among the Lesbia poems, for they express affections which were not alien to the mood of his strong love for her, and reveal the essential singleness of his heart, moved to its depths by a longing for 'friends hid in death's dateless night.' I have written elsewhere in Part II that 'at the root of all his emotional attitudes lay a capacity for affection and an absorption in personal relationships with men and women, which issued in friendship, in sexual love, and in his love of poetry alike—distinctions these, but without a basic emotional difference.' Compare the *Epistle To Allius* (page 39), where memories of brother and mistress are blended.

Multas per gentes et multa per aequora vectus
  Advenio has miseras, frater, ad inferias
Ut te postremo donarem munere mortis
  Et mutam nequiquam adloquerer cinerem.
Quandoquidem fortuna mihi tete abstulit ipsum—
  Heu miser indigne frater adempte mihi.
Nunc tamen interea haec, prisco quae more parentum
  Tradita sunt tristi munere ad inferias,
Accipe fraterno multum manantia fletu,
  Atque in perpetuum, frater, ave atque vale.

HIS BROTHER, we can infer from two passages elsewhere, one of them in the *Epistle To Allius* (page 42), died in Asia and was buried by the Dardanelles, so that the solemn opening of this elegy may well describe that eastward journey from Italy which brought him to the grave, and which, so it is usually conjectured, he undertook when he travelled to Asia Minor in the suite of a provincial governor (page 81).

WORLD WITHOUT END

O'ER many a sea, through many a tribe and nation,
　　　　Brother, I come
To honour thee with mournful salutation
　　　　Paid at thy tomb.
Only this final tribute may I tender
　　　　In grief unheard;
Only address the dust that cannot render
　　　　One answering word.

O thou by fate cut down, dear ghost departed
　　　　In thy first spring,
This age-old office of the broken-hearted
　　　　Behold I bring:
A brother's tearful offerings to cover
　　　　Thy narrow cell,
And his slow-spoken word: Farewell for ever,
　　　　Farewell, farewell.

Si quicquam mutis gratum acceptumve sepulcris
Accidere a nostro, Calve, dolore potest,
Cum desiderio veteres renovamus amores
Atque olim amissas flemus amicitias,
Certe non tanto mors immatura dolori est
Quintiliae, quantum gaudet amore tuo.

SOME of the merits of this epigram are noticed in Part II,
page 141. It has the grave power of the best Greek epitaphs,
yet is written with a more personal emotion than is ever
allowed to appear in them. In the last two lines there is a
balance of syllable and thought, but it is not symmetrical
enough to be mechanical:

tanto . . . is balanced by *quantum* . . . (syntax) and also by
     tuo . . . (assonance);

dolori est . . . is balanced by *gaudet* . . . (antithesis of thought);

mors immatura . . . is balanced by *amore tuo* . . . (assonance plus
     antithesis of thought).

This formalism in the conclusion lends the verse dignity no
less than the sorrowful spondees.

Licinius Calvus, poet and orator and husband of Quintilia, was Jonathan to Catullus' David (page 114). It was a
marriage of true minds, as many of Catullus' verses testify,
and in the imagination of their successors the two men
walked through literary Elysium side by side—'Scholar
Catullus, and your Calvus with you' (page 116). Calvus in
turn had been deeply attached to his wife, and on her death
had written an elegy, a symptom of that romantic revolution
in attitude to sex and marriage which in the last days of the
Republic had overtaken the social and literary clique to
which Catullus belonged, before the imperial regime sought
to put the clock back (page 120). The words '*amore tuo*' may
be meant as a reference to this elegy, which Calvus wrote in
Quintilia's memory, and which she might still enjoy though
dead (page 115).

FOR QUINTILIA DEAD

IF aught of our poor grief has a returning
　　　　To light the dead,
When our old loves come back to us in yearning
　　　　For those long fled,
Then can Quintilia redeem great sorrow
　　　　Of early grave,
Able a greater happiness to borrow
　　　　From your strong love.

IV. THE FLOWER CUT DOWN

THE next long poem forms a remarkable piece of autobiography. It appears to describe some circumstances
under which he had met Lesbia but at what stage it is impos-
slibe to tell. It also lifts the curtain a little on the uneven
happiness which his love for her had brought him. Inter-
twined with these thoughts are bitter memories of his
brother's death. The poem forms a kind of watershed in this
collection. Here the early bliss has given way to disillusionment, though he still strives to accept the situation with
resignation. In the later poems doubt turns to despair and
bitter conflict.

I have imitated only two-thirds of the poem. The original
total of 120 lines is built on an artificial plan, after the worst
Alexandrian manner, with topic enclosing topic like a series
of ingenious caskets (Allius—Lesbia—Laodamia—Troy—
Brother—Troy—Laodamia—Lesbia—Allius). It would
stay unread but for some passages of intense feeling entangled in the formal scheme. These have their own pattern,
but of emotional association, not mechanical theme-struc-
ture. The two sharp thoughts which move him are of Lesbia
half-lost and his brother wholly lost. With these are associated three literary recollections, of Laodamia's love for her
husband, Paris' passion for Helen (treated briefly, but with
significant touches) and Juno's affection for Jove. All three
examples, because of their stories, suggest frustration, even
as his own affections have been frustrated by unfaithfulness
(Lesbia) and by death (brother). It is to be noticed that his
imagination twice selects a woman's figure to symbolize his
own affectionate yearning (cf. Part II, page 118). This series
of rather morbid memories and associations forms as it were
the emotional kernel of the poem. I have accordingly paraphrased the poem in such a way as to extract them and
present them as a loosely-connected chain of lyrical medita-
tions, after the fashion of a fragment of Tennyson's *In
Memoriam*.

Allius, it has been conjectured, may have been one Manlius Torquatus, a literary friend for whom he wrote a marriage-song of unique beauty, but the references in the poem to people, times and places are too ambiguous for anything to be built on them except ingenious guesses (cf. Part II, note 14).

> *Non possum reticere, deae, qua me Allius in re*
>   *Iuverit aut quantis iuverit officiis,*
> *Ne fugiens saeclis obliviscentibus aetas*
>   *Illius hoc caeca nocte tegat studium :*
> 5 *Sed dicam vobis, vos porro dicite multis*
>   *Milibus et facite haec charta loquatur anus.*
>
>   ·   ·   ·   ·   ·
>
> 9 *Nec tenuem texens sublimis aranea telam*
>   *In deserto Alli nomine opus faciat.*
> *Nam mihi quam dederit duplex Amathusia curam*
>   *Scitis, et in quo me corruerit genere,*
> *Cum tantum arderem quantum Trinacria rupes*
>   *Lymphaque in Oetaeis Malia Thermopylis,*
> 15 *Maesta neque adsiduo tabescere lumina fletu*
>   *Cessarent tristique imbre madere genae.*
>
>   ·   ·   ·   ·   ·
>
> 23 *Hic, velut in nigro iactatis turbine nautis*
>   *Lenius adspirans aura secunda venit*
> *Iam prece Pollucis, iam Castoris implorata,*
>   *Tale fuit nobis Allius auxilium.*
> *Is clausum lato patefecit limite campum,*
>   *Isque domum nobis isque dedit dominam;*
> *Ad quam communes exerceremus amores.*
> 30   *Quo mea se molli candida diva pede*
> *Intulit et trito fulgentem in limine plantam*
>   *Innixa arguta constituit solea.*

IN MEMORIAM. AN EPISTLE TO ALLIUS
IN RECORD OF FRIENDSHIP

I

NO more refrain, O muse: declare the story
Of what I owe to Allius my friend.
Immortal may his honour stand defying
The centuries' interminable trend.

Make of my voice a message heard of millions.
Wrinkled let this poor paper still proclaim
The unforgotten service that he rendered.
Let not time's dusty webs surround his name.

II

Thou knowest well how on my heavy spirit
Was laid a double anguish of desire,
How tasting sweets of love I tasted sorrow,
And mingled salt tears with volcanic fire.

Then it was he who ready came to save me,
Like a calm wind to bark by tempest blown.
He lent his house and home for assignation.
So were the barriers to love torn down.

III

At fall of eve my love came to the threshold.
She moved on whispering feet, a goddess fair.
Poised on the trodden stone she stayed her footfall,
Watching me there.

   Coniugis ut quondam flagrans advenit amore
34 *Protesilaeam Laodamia domum*

     . . . .

41 *Coniugis ante coacta novi dimittere collum*
   Quam veniens una atque altera rursus hiems
  Noctibus in longis avidum saturasset amorem,
   Posset ut abrupto vivere coniugio:
45 *Quod scibant Parcae non longo tempore abesse,*
   Si miles muros isset ad Iliacos:
  Nam tum Helenae raptu primores Argivorum
   Coeperat ad sese Troia ciere viros,
  Troia (nefas) commune sepulcrum Asiae Europaeque,
50 *Troia virum et virtutum omnium acerba cinis:*
  Quaene etiam nostro letum miserabile fratri
   Attulit. Hei misero frater adempte mihi,
  Hei misero fratri iucundum lumen ademptum,
   Tecum una tota est nostra sepulta domus,
55 *Omnia tecum una perierunt gaudia nostra,*
   Quae tuus in vita dulcis alebat amor.
  Quem nunc tam longe non inter nota sepulcra
   Nec prope cognatos compositum cineres,
  Sed Troia obscena, Troia infelice sepultum
60 *Detinet extremo terra aliena solo.*
  Ad quam tum properans fertur simul undique pubes
   Graeca penetralis deseruisse focos,
  Ne Paris abducta gavisus libera moecha
   Otia pacato degeret in thalamo.

Her shoe creaked—that was all—and I remembered
Laodamia to her love and lord
Arriving home and waiting in the doorway
       For his first word.

One hour of fellowship they had together,
Ere Trojan service summoned him from home.
So went the gallant flower of Grecian manhood,
Sailing to Troy and their untimely tomb.

IV

Still in that plain are bitter ashes buried.
Alas for Troy! My brother's grave is there.
O brother, how uncomforted your passing:
How dark and comfortless my own despair!

You went, and all the fortunes of our household
Went with you and were buried with your clay,
And my own bliss, that lived by your affection,
       Died in a day.

And now far off in graveyard unfamiliar
Your lonely dust lies in an alien land.
The fateful soil of Troy holds you in keeping,
Laid by the margin of a foreign strand.

V

O dreamer Paris, lying with thy Helen
In stolen bowers of ease, dream thou no more.
The chivalry of Greece, for vengeance hasting,
With arms comes knocking at thy chamber door.

65   *Quo tibi tum casu, pulcherrima Laodamia,*
      Ereptum est ꞌita dulcius atque anima
    Coniugium: tanto te absorbens vertice amoris
      Aestus in abruptum detulerat barathrum

        .   .   .   .   .

77   *Sed tuus altus amor barathro fuit altior illo*
      Qui tunc indomitam ferre iugum docuit.

        .   .   .   .   .

89   *Sed tu horum magnos vicisti sola furores,*
      Ut semel es flavo conciliata viro.
    Aut nihil aut paulo cui tum concedere digna
      Lux mea se nostrum contulit in gremium,
    Quam circumcursans hinc illinc saepe Cupido
      Fulgebat crocina candidus in tunica.
95   *Quae tamenetsi uno non est contenta Catullo,*
      Rara verecundae furta feremus erae,
    Ne nimium simus stultorum more molesti:
      Saepe etiam Iuno, maxima caelicolum,
    Coniugis in culpa flagrantem concoquit iram
100   *Noscens omnivoli plurima furta Iovis.*

        .   .   .   .   .

103   *Nec tamen illa mihi dextra deducta paterna*
      Fragrantem Assyrio venit odore domum,
    Sed furtiva dedit mira munuscula nocte
      Ipsius ex ipso dempta viri gremio.

Laodamia, thou must leave thy lover.
Though thy life go with him, he must depart.
How fathomless the springs of thy affection!
How deep the tides that sweeping fill thy heart!

To bear the yoke of passionate submission
The heart of peerless woman still can learn.
Thy smouldering fires burn on, waiting to kindle
In that brief blissful hour of his return.

VI

Thine image lives again, as now before me
Here in this room another woman stands
Peerless and passionate and proud, yet yielding
   Into my hands.

Light of my life, see where the little Cupid
Clad in his yellow suit, with bow and dart,
Plays hide and seek about us as I clasp you
   Close to my heart.

VII

What though my love alone cannot content her?
She is discreet; her sins none other sees.
Why play the jealous fool? The queen of heaven
Herself must bear Jove's infidelities.

No flare of torches brought her to my dwelling;
No marriage-escort might her journey mark.
Stolen from husband's bed were her caresses,
The secrets murmured in the magic dark.

107   *Quare illud satis est, si nobis is datur unis*
         Quem lapide illa diem candidiore notat.

       Hoc tibi quod potui confectum carmine munus
110   *Pro multis, Alli, redditur officiis,*
       Ne vestrum scabra tangat robigine nomen
           Haec atque illa dies atque alia atque alia.
       Huc addent divi quam plurima, quae Themis olim
           Antiquis solita est munera ferre piis:
115   *Sitis felices et tu simul et tua vita*
           Et domus, in qua nos lusimus et domina,

                    .   .   .   .   .
119   *Et longe ante omnes mihi quae me carior ipso est,*
           Lux mea, qua viva vivere dulce mihi est.

Of all her golden days can she remember
Some with a special quality of bliss?
Let her keep these for me. My short petition
        Asks only this.

VIII

Allius, sterling friend, my verse is ended
Which celebrates your service and your praise.
May fleet tomorrow's day and then tomorrow
Never your monument with rust erase.

The gods are just, and ever have rewarded
Men of true heart and faithful to their oath.
May you and she you love enjoy their blessing:
        Peace to you both.

Peace to that house of memories immortal
In spring time of our love that saw us meet,
Peace above all to that dear life that renders
        My own life sweet.

THE ten remaining poems are all unhappy. They show how impossible he found it to sustain that mood of tolerant resignation in which he had been able to compare himself to the patient wife of Jove. First come two reproachful epigrams, upbraiding her for broken promises:

> *Iucundum, mea vita, mihi proponis amorem*
> *Hunc nostrum inter nos perpetuumque fore.*
> *Di magni, facite ut vere promittere possit*
> *Atque id sincere dicat et ex animo,*
> *Ut liceat nobis tota perducere vita*
> *Aeternum hoc sanctae foedus amicitiae.*

ONE WORD PROFANED

AND would you give a love that shall be dear
    And never die—
Our love? Ah, God, give her a heart sincere
    That cannot lie,
And lips whose promises are something worth
    Nor lightly told,
That love and happiness be ours on earth
    To have and hold.

IN form this verse, with its repetition of *dicit* and its demand that woman's vows be written in water, recalls conceits favoured by the poets of the Greek Silver Age, and as old as Sophocles. But the rather unpretentious way in which Catullus has expressed this threadbare theme achieves a sincerity which the Alexandrian versions are too pretty and ingenious to manage (page 142).

> *Nulli se dicit mulier mea nubere malle*
> *Quam mihi, non si se Iuppiter ipse petat.*
> *Dicit, sed mulier cupido quod dicit amanti*
> *In vento et rapida scribere oportet aqua.*

One commentator dismisses the verse as a jest, while another interprets it as a 'reproach for having broken the definite pledge of marriage'. Surely, however, it is possible to take the verse seriously without taking it literally (Part II, page 83).

WOMAN'S FAITH

MY lady says, None other would she marry
          But only me;
  Not Jove himself, a suitor though he tarry,
          Yea, even He.
  She says—but what a lady to her lover
          Softly may say—
  Write it upon the wind or in the river
          That pass for aye.

THE next five are poems of conflict. They dramatize with painful intensity his own desperate struggle with himself to give her up, and as examples of self-revelation are surely unique in poetry. First comes this poignant soliloquy, written, like the *Salute to Sirmio*, in limping iambics, but with how different a content!

> *Miser Catulle, desinas ineptire*
> *Et quod vides perisse perditum ducas.*
> *Fulsere quondam candidi tibi soles*
> *Cum ventitabas quo puella ducebat*
> *Amata nobis quantum amabitur nulla.*
> *Ibi illa multa tum iocosa fiebant,*
> *Quae tu volebas nec puella nolebat.*
> *Fulsere vere candidi tibi soles.*
> *Nunc iam illa non vult: tu quoque, impotens, noli,*
> *Nec quae fugit sectare, nec miser vive,*
> *Sed obstinata mente perfer, obdura.*
> *Vale, puella! iam Catullus obdurat,*
> *Nec te requiret nec rogabit invitam:*
> *At tu dolebis, cum rogaberis nulla.*
> *Scelesta, vae te! quae tibi manet vita!*
> *Quis nunc te adibit? cui videberis bella?*
> *Quem nunc amabis? cuius esse diceris?*
> *Quem basiabis? cui labella mordebis?*
> *At tu, Catulle, destinatus obdura.*

The lines reveal striking powers both of imagination and of poetic construction. The loss which he imagines for her is really his own; by a trick of identification, he has projected himself into her (Part II, page 119) and has then chosen to express this emotion in a dainty metrical form converted to the service of tragedy. His successors in Latin poetry turned their backs on this experiment. (Compare the essay on *Lyric and Liberty* in Part II.)

MISER CATULLE

POOR poet, let your folly sleep:
The past is dead: bury it deep.
Time was your love neath sunny sky
Beckoned to you as she went by,
And your fond merriment could stir
An equal happiness in her.
The passion that you lent her then
Mocked the mere loves of common men.
Sunny the skies, and every day
Was summer—till she turned away.

Turn from her then yourself, nor strive
In futile misery to live.
Pursue no more the hope that flies:
No more remember love that dies.
Be resolute: make your heart hard—
Goodbye, my dear: I've said the word.
My heart is steeled, my love shall sleep,
Nor seek the kiss you'd rather keep.

But you when heart and hand forsake—
Yours is the hard heart that will break.
Who will make love when I am gone?
Call you his dear, his fair, his own?
Where's the heart now your heart adores?
Whose lips shall print themselves on yours
And leave their mark on them?—But stay!
Turn from her, poet, turn away.

ODI ET AMO—such is the paradox which furnishes theme for the next three epigrams, and is tersely expressed in the third of them. The first, of four lines, finds verbal echo in the second, of eight. The two thus form a corresponding pair, both of them excellent illustrations of that facility for compressing strong emotion into meticulous forms, which is so characteristic of his genius (Part II, page 137).

Huc est mens deducta tua, mea Lesbia, culpa,
Atque ita se officio perdidit ipsa suo,
Ut iam nec bene velle queat tibi, si optima fias,
Nec desistere amare, omnia si facias.

THE OFFICE OF MY HEART

THE office of my heart is still to love
      When I would hate.
Time and again your faithlessness I prove
      Proven too late.
Your ways might mend, yet my contempt could never
      Be now undone.
Yet crimes repeated cannot stop this fever
      From burning on.

Dicebas quondam solum te nosse Catullum,
  Lesbia, nec prae me velle tenere Iovem.
Dilexi tum te non tantum ut vulgus amicam,
  Sed pater ut gnatos diligit et generos.
Nunc te cognovi: quare etsi impensius uror,
  Multo mi tamen es vilior et levior.
Qui potis est? inquis. Quod amantem iniuria talis
  Cogit amare magis, sed bene velle minus.

WE HAVE seen already how his love-poetry breathes a
most un-Roman romanticism. In lines three and four of this
piece, this feeling seems to transcend itself. Surely no other
poet of antiquity, and few in any age, would have committed
themselves to a confession of such pure and almost impersonal affection. Yet need it therefore be dismissed as incredible? (Part II, pages 85, 148).

THE UNDYING FIRE

ONCE you would say to me: 'Your heart has found me
                And yours alone.
I would not have the arms of Jove around me
                More than your own'.
Saying it, you became no more the fashion
                Of cheap desire,
But wife and child and home, loved with the passion
                Of life-long fire.

I know you now   Yet my soul goes on burning,
                As burn it must,
When you and all I gave to you are turning
                To death and dust.
Strange, do you say? How strange that love should cherish
                Light that is gone!
That every kindly thought of you should perish,
                Yet love last on.

Odi et amo. Quare id faciam fortasse requiris.
Nescio. Sed fieri sentio, et excrucior.

THESE are the words of barest prose, and placed in prose order. The couplet indeed is scarcely poetry in the usual sense of that word. On the one hand it avoids appealing to the imagination through image and symbol; on the other it refuses to end with the neat point proper to epigram. Its poetic power, if it has one, consists in defying the arts of poetry.

BONDAGE

I LOATHE her, and I love her. 'Can I show
    How both should be?'
I loathe and love, and nothing else I know
    But agony.

IN THIS the last of the five poems of conflict he again engages in dialogue with himself, as he did in the first (*Miser Catulle*). But the conflict has grown more desperate, and now an appeal to heaven seems to reduce him to a state of emotional exhaustion: let her abandon him if she must; all he wants is peace of mind, at any price:

> *Si qua recordanti benefacta priora voluptas*
> *Est homini, cum se cogitat esse pium,*
> *Nec sanctam violasse fidem, nec foedere in ullo*
> *Divum ad fallendos numine abusum homines,*
> 5   *Multa parata manent in longa aetate, Catulle,*
> *Ex hoc ingrato gaudia amore tibi.*
> *Nam quaecumque homines bene cuiquam aut dicere possunt*
> *Aut facere, haec a te dictaque factaque sunt:*
> *Omnia quae ingratae perierunt credita menti.*
> 10   *Quare cur tu te iam amplius excrucies?*
> *Quin tu animo offirmas atque istinc teque reducis*
> *Et dis invitis desinis esse miser?*
> *Difficile est longum subito deponere amorem:*
> *Difficile est, verum hoc qua libet efficias.*
> 15   *Una salus haec est, hoc est tibi pervincendum:*
> *Hoc facias, sive id non pote sive pote.*
> *O di, si vestrum est misereri, aut si quibus unquam*
> *Extremam iam ipsa in morte tulistis opem,*
> *Me miserum adspicite et, si vitam puriter egi,*
> 20   *Eripite hanc pestem perniciemque mihi!*

JOURNEY'S END

THEY say that benefits to others rendered
 Win in our memories their late reward.
They say that love, once it is loyally tendered,
 Stays sweet and keeps the lover's heart unscarred.

If it is true that faith promised and given
 Is profit, and a guileless heart is gain,
How surely shall I prosper, who have striven
  So long with pain.

The gentle word, the generous intent,
 The decent things that men can do or say,
All these to gladden her I freely spent,
 But could not touch her when she turned away.

Why then, you fool, cherish your long affliction?
 Why fight against the thing that must prevail?
Put her away from you. Need resolution
  For ever fail?

'It is impossible to lay aside for ever
 In one brief point of time the love of years.'
Then do th' impossible. Steel yourself. Sever
 This knot, and wring relief from bitter tears.

O gods, if yours be pity, yours compassion
 Given to failing men even on the road
Leading to death, dispel this black obsession,
 Rescue my soul from hell. Support its load—

> *Hei mihi subrepens imos ut torpor in artus*
> *Expulit ex omni pectore laetitias.*
> *Non iam illud quaero, contra ut me diligat illa,*
> *Aut, quod non potis est, esse pudica velit:*
> 25 *Ipse valere opto et taetrum hunc deponere morbum.*
> *O di, reddite mi hoc pro pietate mea!*

These thirteen couplets compose a powerful poem because of the way in which they manage to reflect the ebb and flow of his mental struggle. The emotional tension alters, but the mood remains a continuous stream:

> lines 1–8 sorrowful reflection, passing, 9–12, into mental struggle:
>
> 13 relapse, followed, 14–16, by renewed struggle, and 17–20, a cry for help:
>
> 21–22 relapse into stupor (this passage receives a complete English stanza to itself):
>
> 23-24 resignation, rising, 25–26, to a last outburst.

This alternation projects the drama of his mind so effectively as to suggest some mime in which the actor performs the violent gestures of struggle and exhaustion.

It is related of Macaulay that parts of the poem could move him to tears. It has one lapse from poetry (*haec a te dictaque factaque sunt*, an attempt at the prose-poetry style; cf. pages 30, 58 above). He is in effect expanding the epigram into a vehicle of sustained reflection, and the poem is thus the forerunner of the elegy as it was perfected by Ovid, Propertius and Tibullus.

The remarkable opening lines, which recall the 'benefits forgot' with philosophic melancholy, reflect the singleness of his emotions. Love was not a separate category from friendship (Part II, page 114).

How like a stupor every sense pervading
 My sorrow steals! How faint I grow with grief!
How swift the sunlight of my life is fading,
   My bliss how brief!

I look no more for her to be my lover
As I love her. That thing could never be.
No ɔray I for her purity—that's over.
Only this much I pray, that I be free,

Free from insane desire myself, and guarded
In peace at last. O heaven, grant that yet
The faith by which I've lived may be rewarded.
   Let me forget.

Caeli, Lesbia nostra, Lesbia illa,
Illa Lesbia, quam Catullus unam
Plus quam se atque suos amavit omnes
Nunc in quadriviis at angiportis
Glubit magnanimi Remi nepotes.

THE VERSE reads like a cry of anguish. In *Lesbia nostra, Lesbia illa, Illa Lesbia* the word terminations beat like a throb of pain, an effect impossible in an uninflected tongue. So I have replaced the reiteration by some touches of physical detail, so conspicuous by their absence in his poetry.

The third line conveys a pathos which it is easy to miss: he had violated tradition by loving a mere woman more than family and friends. And now, having allowed his romanticism to carry him away, he has left himself defenceless;

In the last untranslatable line, bitter obscenity is redeemed with just a hint of historical glamour to point an ironic contrast: the men she accosts at the street corner are heirs to the Roman pride.

It has been conjectured that he wrote this verse after learning of the revelations about Clodia's private life made by Cicero in the speech in which he attacked her in order to defend his client Caelius Rufus, who would thus be the *Caelius* of this poem. (Part II, page 81.) If this be true, then separation must have made him very morbid, if he could thus take the innuendoes of a hostile lawyer as evidence against her.

SHE THAT I LOVED

SHE that I loved, that face,
   Those hands, that hair,
Dearer than all my race,
   As dear as fair—
See her where throngs parade
   Th'imperial route,
Plying her skill unpaid—
   Rome's prostitute.

Furi et Aureli, comites Catulli,
Sive in extremos penetrabit Indos
Litus ut longe resonante Eoa
      Tunditur unda,

Sive in Hyrcanos Arabasve molles,
Seu Sacas sagittiferosve Parthos,
Sive quae septemgeminus colorat
      Aequora Nilus,

Sive trans altas gradietur Alpes
Caesaris visens monimenta magni,
Gallicum Rhenum, horribile aequor, ulti-
      mosque Britannos,

Omnia haec, quaecunque feret voluntas
Caelitum, temptare simul parati,
Pauca nuntiate meae puellae
      Non bona dicta:

Cum suis vivat valeatque moechis,
Quos simul complexa tenet trecentos
Nullum amans vere, sed identidem omnium
      Ilia rumpens;

Nec meum respectet, ut ante, amorem,
Qui illius culpa cecidit velut prati
Ultimi flos, praetereunte postquam
      Tactus aratro est.

These verses blend personal emotion with historical romance
(Part II, pp. 128, 179). Like the *Bid Me To Live*, they are written in Sapphics; an archaic metre lends dignity to his renunciation, as it had to his early adoration. There is irony in the
comites Catulli ('born companions, forsooth!') and their pretentious promises (*omnia haec*, etc.) contrasted with the service
actually required (*panuca non bona dicta*). As for the blossom
touched by the plough, that too is ironic, but in a different
sense (page 111).

THE LAST WORD

FRIENDS, who profess your ardour to explore
  The ends of earth with me, on India's shore
The long wave breaking calls for evermore
        Clamorously:

Wide are the steppes and wild the Russian land:
His plains the Parthian ranges bow in hand:
Dark flows the Nile, dyeing the sea and sand
        Eternally:

Steep rise the Alpine roads that Caesar's host
Climbed to accomplish his imperial boast—
Gaul and the Rhineland and wild Britain's coast
        Afar removed:

You are prepared, you say, for each reverse
Of fate. But can you welcome something worse?
Dare you convey a last compendious curse
        To her I loved?

Tell her: God speed you, lady, to your bed,
Where thousand lovers lie there lay your head,
Promising love to them give lust instead,
        False to the core:

Tell her how love, that in my heart one day
Blossomed unbidden as a wildflower may,
The scythe has caught, and she can throw away
        What blooms no more.

Male est, Cornifici, tuo Catullo,
Male est me hercule et ei laboriose,
Et magis magis in dies et horas.
Quem tu, quod minimum facillimumque est,
Qua solatus es adlocutione!
Irascor tibi! Sic meos amores?
Paulum quid libet adlocutionis,
Maestius lacrimis Simonideis.

THESE lines reveal a sensitive emotional temper which chooses to express itself in an idiom both colloquial and cultivated. In eight brief eleven-syllables he has written what is almost an elegy. Such is the mood and style of the *homo urbanus, venustus* (Part II, pp. 102, 111). Cornificius was probably himself a contemporary poet of the same school as claimed Catullus's allegiance, a school which demanded above all things those elegant qualities foreshadowed in the dedication, and which appear also here in the conclusion. The poem is an appeal to a fellow-poet to return lyrical consolation, and *paulum quid libet* rather indicates that Catullus hoped for an equally artless reply in similar metre. Yet he touches his slight composition with the glamour of the great archaic school of Greek lyric. In grief he thinks of Simonides, as in love he had thought of Sappho.

We can guess if we choose that his melancholy conveys a premonition of his own death, as untimely as apparently his brother's had been. At any rate, the verse reads like a milestone announcing that the end of his emotional career is at hand; so it is placed here to conclude the story of his love.

SWAN SONG

THIS ailing friend of yours
   Is sadly scarred.
The day is dark, and oh
   The way grows hard,
And harder every hour
   Of every day.
And you—had you one word
   Of cheer to say?
A light and little thing
   It were to spare:
You make me wild! Is this
   All that you care?
Just one small word to soothe
   My lonely fears,
Sad as Simonides'
   Melodious tears.

PART II

ANALYSIS OF
THE CATULLAN TEMPER

THE CANONS OF CATULLAN
CRITICISM

THE memory of Catullus' poetry was nearly as frail as his life. He wrote in the last days of the Roman republic. Within a generation the landmarks of republicanism had been swept away in civil war, and when the imperial system rose upon the ruins, there arose with it the literary movement of the Augustan age, committed to the task of creating a new poetry to match the new edifice of government. The kind of occasional lyrics that Catullus wrote had no place in this official sort of literature, and though he left his impress on Virgil's youthful mind, though Propertius, Statius, Martial imitated him, and others like Ovid and the younger Pliny remembered him gratefully, he was honoured sparingly in the empire. He was not the sort of poet to be readily embalmed in a school-book. His verses, though they included a few ambitious pieces, were on the whole neither pretentious nor moral; they were read but not revered. And he fared worse as time went on. For five hundred years he seems to have been practically forgotten, and we might know little of him but his name if the solitary manuscript on which all our texts depend had not been discovered in mysterious fashion at his birthplace of Verona at the beginning of the fourteenth century. To this day his fate continues. His one hundred and eighteen poems fail to constitute a good discipline for the class-room. Some of them are obscene, many more are too slight in their occasion and substance, the total is very uneven in quality, and his best verse excels because it breathes a lyrical enthusiasm alien (alas!) to the professed methods of education, which for its own purposes pretends that in the class-room the heart does not exist. So he remains on the fringe of Latin letters as they are to-day taught and interpreted.

Scholarship however has during the last century spent much pains upon him, and whether because of its labours, or that there is something in the modern mood which responds to Catullus and prizes the intense personal experience of his poetry above the elaborate art of Virgil or Horace, his muse begins to receive honour in diverse and unexpected quarters. A lively discussion of public affairs was recently published in England, which in the form of a dialogue offered various opinions on such assorted topics as raw materials, Fascism, and the gold standard.[1] In the conclusion occurs the following hopeful paragraph: 'There is a good deal of English laughter going on, and a certain number of people reading Catullus.'

'Why is Catullus so important?' asked Algernon.

'Because no one could possibly pretend that he was a Fascist or a Communist or belonged to the Right or belonged to the Left, or indeed was anything in the world but just a damned good poet, worth reading for the fun of the sound.'

There are only a hundred and eighteen[2] poems and fragments of his to read. These appear in all the standard editions in an order which follows the manuscript arrangement. First, sixty short poems written in assorted metres, the majority in eleven-syllables ('hendecasyllabics,' so called from the length of each line) and iambics (two varieties). Both of these metres read easily and swiftly. Then come a group of nine (the last two of which appear as one in the MS.) in four varieties of metre. These poems bisect the collection and owe their position solely to their length. The shortest has forty-eight lines and the longest four hundred and eight. Following them come forty-nine short verses written in elegiacs and normally labelled epigrams, a traditional but misleading title. The total arrangement is thus purely formal; such a mechanical method of division could scarcely have been adopted till some time after the poet's death. On the one hand it pays no regard to the poetic substance of the verses, nor on the other does it attempt, presumably, to reproduce their chronology.[3]

This then being the brief memorial through which Catullus survives to posterity, how shall its significance be interpreted? Surely the first canon of criticism would be the negative one, that we should not expect such a formal arrangement of the poems to reveal anything of the poet. It divides him into three parts: Are these parts real? Do they represent different aspects of his genius? Even a cursory reading soon reveals that the manuscript, by reserving all the epigrams to the end, disguises their close connection with the first group of short verses, from which they are not essentially different in mood, style or substance. Catullus in fact composed a mass of short verse which can be sub-divided into (a) lampoons and humorous pieces, (b) emotional lyrics which run the whole gamut of the feelings, love, hate, joy, grief, despair. For both these varieties of verse he used several metres but especially the eleven-syllable, the iambic, and the 'epigrammatic,' if I may so term the elegiac metre when used in short verse. The total of a hundred and nine poems and fragments deserves to be regarded as a single body of work displaying certain common characteristics of style and substance, the work in fact of a lyric poet.

What then of the nine longer poems? The fact that they occur as an isolated group tempts the reader to assume that they represent a separate aspect of the poet's genius. Such indeed is the hypothesis which colours most scholastic criticism of him, based on the fact that in the first place they cannot be lyrics because they are too long, and in the second place they betray considerable artifice in their structure and learning in their content. Hence they have been taken to represent in particular that tendency to erudition and elaboration of style which Catullus is supposed to have imitated in current Roman fashion from the Greek poets of Alexandria. We are thus continually tempted to believe in two Catulluses, a lyrist given to the composition of spontaneous and artless verse, and a formal poet who deliberately sets out to acquire those elaborate arts of poetic construction which were suggested by the example of Alexandria, and which the Augustan poets brought to perfection.

Now it is on *a priori* grounds risky to assume that a poet's muse can be thus partitioned. There have been poets—for example, Burns—who wrote in two such different styles and personalities as Catullus is supposed to have written in. But Catullus was no Burns, though the comparison is often made; he was no ploughman's son with a gift for popular song and a desire to improve himself by learning the mannerisms of the metropolis. Rome could not have infected Catullus with sophistication as Edinburgh infected Burns, for he was sophisticated already. The habit of dividing the poet into two personalities is fatal to Catullan criticism, for it obscures the true quality of his lyrics. It prevents us from noticing that where they appear most spontaneous, they are also most sophisticated; that his emotional sincerity is coloured by a romantic feeling for 'gods dethroned and empires of the past'; that so far from possessing a naïve and untutored gift of expression which later yields to scholarship and Alexandrian affectation, he reveals himself scholar, wit and sophisticate from first to last.

The same error has sometimes prevented his longer poems from being judged in their true perspective. Classify them from the point of view of poetic significance, and we find in the first place two with no poetic significance at all. Of these one, the *Dialogue With a Door* (No. 67), reads like an adolescent experiment.[4] It seems to be an attack on the morals of some local married woman, but it is both feeble and obscure. The other (66), a mannered and involved translation from the Greek of Callimachus' ingenious poem *Berenice's Lock of Hair*, is a piece of hack-work written to order.[5] Neither of these poems has anything to contribute to our understanding of Catullus, unless it be the knowledge that he could write as indifferently as any other poet when he chose. Another poem, a choral marriage-song (62), also reads like a fairly close imitation of some Greek original, though it has some pretty passages. Then there are the three versified epistles (65, 68a, 68b) addressed to friends. Each of them considered as a whole is a complete failure, lacking unity and even emotional direction, but each contains a few remarkable passages, either bursts of self-revelation written with direct sincerity or purple patches of spasmodic beauty.[6] The last of the three, the *Epistle to Allius*, tries to impose on the epistolary style the structure of an epic romance and turn the poem into a 'little epic' (epyllion).[7] Never was there such dismal failure of form to master matter. But its frequent lapses from pretentious mythology into personal revelation will always make the poem memorable, which is why two-thirds of it is included in Part I. This brings us to his one whole-hearted essay in the epic style—the famous *Peleus and Thetis* (64), an epyllion in what is recognized as the Alexandrian manner. Now as a literary event this poem of 408 lines was undoubtedly significant, because of its profound influence as a model for his Augustan successors, the true 'Alexandrians'. But what is its significance as a part of his own poetry? Again the epic construction breaks down. The poem is read for the emotional episodes and semi-lyrical passages that it contains—Ariadne gazing distraught from the Cretan shore like a statue in stone—her passionate lament—the flowers brought to Peleus' wedding—the refrain chanted by the three fates. These are strung together with a minimum of hasty narrative into an ill-assorted series.[8] So, finally, we pass to his two indubitable successes in sustained poetic composition, the *Marriage Song For Manlius and Vinia* (61), and the *Emasculation of Attis* (63). If these stand unique in Latin poetry, it is because, with their rapid metre and breathless mood, they are simply long sustained lyrics. The *Attis* discards all the mythological learning which the commentators hasten to supply in their notes; its hero simply sails across the sea with a chosen band to perform the dreadful rite upon himself, and the setting having been thus perfunctorily sketched in the first five lines, the poem devotes itself to his frenzied dash to Ida's summit, his exhaustion, sleep, revival, remorse, and final terror. As for the *Bridal Song*, it makes us dance as we read, dazzling our senses with a succession of vivid images—Vinia like a myrtle blossom with the dew on it—the torches like hair aflame—the bridegroom like a vine clasped to his bride—lifting her across the threshold—their ten thousand joys (like Lesbia's kisses)—the baby son.

The conclusion is plain; Catullus, if he is to be read as a poet, and not simply classified and labelled like some figure in a literary museum, should be interpreted first and last as a lyrist.[9] Even in his longer compositions, his writing becomes significant and important only in so far as it is lyrical. He is *par excellence* the poet of intense moods, expressed either singly or in rapid succession.[10] This it is true requires poetic organization, but the organization is of the emotions pure and simple. Let him pause to reflect, to marshal ideas or situations which call for an effort of abstraction, and his muse fails. But, let us again repeat, his lyric is of a peculiar kind, sophisticated, complex, highly civilized, and capable, as will later appear, of deft and even precise handling of its own appropriate and sometimes traditional forms. If we are to comprehend Catullus, the two pictures, of the naïve emotionalist and the scholar-intellectual, have to be combined into a single mental portrait. The division of him into two personalities[11] has to be discarded. It is irreconcilable with the spirit of his significant poetry.

To enlarge our understanding of what Catullus wrote, scholarship has spent considerable pains upon the task of reconstructing the events of his short life. Nothing in the present fashion of literature seems more natural. The great ones of to-day have their biographers who like literary undertakers only wait for the decease in order to complete and publish the life. The increase of reading has spread a vague consciousness of history in the minds of multitudes, such as probably never existed before, and this has happened just at a time when the science of psychology had begun to teach the importance of early environment and to trace conscious thought and action to unexpected sources. The result has been that the twin forces of history and psychology have united to produce a school of literary criticism which believes that the poetry of Shakespeare or the philosophy of Plato are best understood against a factual background of biography, which can relate the artist's work to his early education and career in the world, his friends and travels, domestic history and commercial dealings.

Catullus' verses would at first sight appear to lend themselves very well to this method of biographical criticism. He is the most personal poet of antiquity. Of the sixty lyrics and fragments which form the first part of his book, only two, a *Hymn to Diana* and a little love-drama, the *Acme and Septimius*, are detached from the immediate occasions of his daily life. Forty-six of them begin by addressing in the vocative case some person or thing, whether friend or enemy, Lesbia's sparrow, his writing paper, or himself. Scholarship, not being slow to take advantage of this poetic habit, has sought to marshal these references in some sort of chronological sequence, combining them with the current history of the times to form a biography of the poet.

The result is an elaborate structure of ingenious hypotheses. *We may suppose* (so runs the reconstructed story in its most complete form)[12] that Catullus spent his boyhood at Verona and on Lake Sirmio, a youth of good provincial family, but, *we must assume*, living a life close to that of the Gallic frontiersmen. His education, *no doubt* received at Verona, was, *we can readily imagine*, assisted by tutors and grammarians of the district—we hear elsewhere of several who taught in Cisalpine Gaul at about this period[20]—who could teach him that knowledge and love of Greek poetry so manifest in his verse. At Verona (*it is tempting to assume*) he was introduced to Metellus, the husband of his future love, during Metellus' governorship of Cisalpine Gaul in 62 B.C. Armed (*we may imagine*) with letters of introduction, he comes, a young unsophisticated provincial, to the capital, meets Clodia (if he had not met her already), his superior in years and station, and falls violently in love with her. For a period he worships her from afar, expressing his emotion in his more romantic love-lyrics. With her assistance, however, (*it is safe to guess*) he obtains entry, despite his provincialism, to the most exclusive circles of fashion and politics in Rome, thus achieving personal relationships which he again proceeds to reveal in his verse. By the year 60 (*we may perhaps infer*) his love had been declared and consummated at the house and with the assistance of one Manlius Torquatus, subsequently thanked in a long and largely obscure poem. (This is the *Epistle to Allius*, imitated in Part I.[14]) It was a fleeting happiness he thus enjoyed. His brother died (*probably*) next year (59); the loss may well have clouded the rest of his life. Revisiting Verona, *doubtless* to console his parents, he hears of Clodia's infidelities, and refers to them rather vaguely, in another versified epistle. Her husband however had died, so (*no doubt* about this time) Catullus asked her (*we infer* from one epigram) to marry him. But she preferred a life of pleasurable freedom, at Rome and at Baiae the watering-place, enjoying various lovers, among them one Caelius

Rufus, soon bitterly recognized and attacked by the poet as his chief rival. *About this time* also (*we must assume*), responding to advice from elder and graver leaders of literature like the orator Hortensius and Manlius Torquatus, he essayed a more learned and Alexandrian manner, deserting his earlier simplicity to attempt some longer and more elaborate poems, meanwhile maintaining a running fire of political and personal lampoons directed specially against Caesar, Pompey and Caesar's lieutenants. By 58 his love for Clodia had (*probably*) died; at any rate none of his love lyrics can be shown to post-date this year. In 57 he joined the suite of the proconsul for the province of Asia for that year, visited his brother's grave, and (*if we can assume* the poem on *The Old Yacht* to be autobiographical) sailed home to Sirmio in a private yacht purchased in Asia. This Eastern journey (*we may imagine*) encouraged his experiments in mythological verse and romantic idyll in the Alexandrian manner. Meanwhile Rufus, after quarrelling with Clodia, had become involved in a prosecution which she assisted herself; Cicero as defending counsel counter-attacked by blackening Clodia's character as much as he could. Therefore (*we can guess*) that Catullus on his return must have learnt these secrets of Clodia's private life revealed in court[15] (56 B.C.). The fresh shock (*no doubt*) helped to inspire his last address to her in 55, an address (*perhaps*) provoked by a request from her for a reconciliation. In this poem (page 66) he stated that his love is already dead. However, its complimentary references to Caesar's conquests in Gaul and Britain *lead us to believe* that in the realm of politics he had by this time accomplished a reconciliation with the dictator of Gaul. He must have died a few months later.

I have given this hypothetical biography for what it is worth. At least half of it may well be correct; but it remains hypothetical, a structure of probables and possibles, cemented by *we may well imagine* and *it is safe to infer*. Its foundations are flimsy. To give one example, it has to make use of the attack which Cicero in his speech *Pro Caelio* launched against Clodia in order to defend Caelius Rufus. Yet we happen to know that Cicero had once pondered the possibility of divorcing his own wife in order to marry Clodia! Was the lover or the lawyer in him the more reliable witness to her virtues? However, the flimsiness is not the trouble. A biography only half-correct in detail may yet, by placing the poet in his times and circumstances, endow him with flesh and blood and make him intelligible. But biography built up in this way is always in danger of being over-literal in its use of evidence. The critic if he allows his method to run away with him may by degrees find himself constructing a character for his poet, inferred from the supposed 'facts' of his life, which becomes a sort of strait jacket into which the literary remains have somehow to be fitted. Biographical criticism, in brief, may be allowed to override the evidence of literary criticism, with disastrous results, and in Catullus' case we have a striking example of this error.

In obedience to the historical method, we are asked to suppose that, merely because he was born in Verona in 'the province',[16] he therefore came to Rome a raw provincial, a young poet of naïve and untutored enthusiasm, compelled to gain access only by degrees to the fringe of Rome's social and literary cliques, the queenly Clodia condescending to be his sponsor. To assume this we have to ignore the fact that his verse deals familiarly with all the chief literary and political figures of his day, and moreover in its most lyrical mood manages to convey an urban assurance, in a collo-quial yet fashionable idiom which I shall later attempt to analyse. It echoes with careless ease not only the small talk of smart dinner-tables but also the sophisticated endear-ments of civilized love and friendship. Clearly his inferior social status exists only in the imagination of some scholars, and this 'provincial hypothesis' has prevented a proper appreciation of his poetic style.

In many ways a habit of factual literalness may inhibit true critical imagination. For example, in the famous eleventh poem, the Sapphic in which he renounces Lesbia for ever (page 66), there is a complimentary reference to Caesar's conquests in Gaul. The biographical method, mindful of other verses in which Catullus attacks Caesar, proceeds to explain the present reference in terms of a supposed reconciliation between the two men, using a hint in Suetonius to assist this hypothesis.[17] Now, such a reconciliation may or may not have occurred, but to thrust it forward here is to give an entirely false emphasis to the poem, representing it as a compliment to Caesar, instead of as an achievement of the creative imagination. The poetic reason for inserting such a verse is its flavour of romance—the contemporary romance of empire-building—and this is only part of a skilful poetic construction which in the total poem lends an effect of solemn and impersonal dignity to his bitter parting (cf. page 128 below). A poet might continue to detest Napoleon, shall we say, yet allow himself to romanticize his victories.

This kind of criticism has done particular violence to Catullus' love-poetry. It has demanded that as far as possible such poetry should be explained in terms of some occasion or circumstance rather than of the poet's own powerful and subjective imagination. For example, the mood of *Bid Me To Live* (page 12), because it worships his mistress from afar, is taken as evidence of his inferior social status to hers, as though adoration in love were nicely proportioned to the lady's comparative income and eminence. Again, if the poet cries

> My lady says 'None other would she marry
> But only me' etc.,

this, we are told, must mean a literal proposal of marriage, therefore of course the husband was dead when this was written. But does the language of love ever yield to such literal application? Could she not cry to him in the night 'I'd rather marry you than all the world' without having posterity accuse her of feminine breach of promise? The truth is that the critic, instead of allowing his sympathy to grasp the mood and form of these luckless lyrics, is always laying ambushes for them, from which he may rush out and surprise the poet in the act of betraying some beggarly item of chronology. So we are asked to accept one poem as the result of a quarrel, and another as the result of a reconciliation, and so forth. Such explanations of his poetry are not only flimsy in themselves; they distract attention from its essential element—the subjective intensity of the poet's immediate feeling. In Part I his love lyrics have been arranged purely formally, according to their mood. What their chronology was we shall never know. An eminent Catullan critic truly remarks of *Reunion* (page 30), 'It is mere trifling to fix the period at which it was written', and another as eminent refuses to date *Journey's End* (page 60), 'so fiercely vacillating were the moods of the poet's mind'.[18] Such judgments can safely be applied to most of the love-poetry.

Generally, it may be said that Catullan criticism in these matters is continually in danger of betraying a certain vulgarity of feeling, a failure of taste. Perhaps this is because Catullus alone of Latin and indeed all ancient poets that survive has left poetry which is too intensely subjective to submit at all readily to the methods of measurement which classical scholarship is prone to adopt. He is too 'modern.' Because one of his verses demands a million kisses, and another answers her question How many do you want?, scholarship, presumably in the interests of symmetry, has gone so far as to assert that 'in number five the basia are given *by* Lesbia, in seven *to* her; a subjective and objective statement of the same circumstance, which has not been observed'.[19] It does not seem to have occurred to the commentator that when lovers kiss, distinction between subject and object may become a little difficult to draw. There is a romanticism, an attitude of spiritual surrender, infusing much of his verse which has proved well-nigh incomprehensible to the critics, and measured by ancient standards it is. In the verse *My True Love Hath My Heart* (page 26) he is content to express his purely one-sided devotion to her. Merely because of this fact, apparently, scholarship has taken it to be an incomplete fragment, and asks us to suppose that there once existed a missing half which must have portrayed by contrast her own unfaithfulness to him. But why thus grudge the lover his generous adoration, however illogical and foolish? So strong indeed was the romanticism in his temper that he could go the length of writing

> In those days I loved you not so much as the common
> herd love a mistress
>
> But as a father loves his children . . .

To the critic's way of thinking, this does not make sense: one does not love one's mistress as a father his child. So we are asked to believe that these lines represent a fumbling and confused attempt to express his naïve bewilderment at his own love. There are plenty of modern lovers ready to testify that the beloved can be passionately desired, yet with the protective affection with which a father 'pitieth his children', but Catullus apparently is to be denied this emotional privilege.

Such animadversions upon certain aspects of contemporary Catullan criticism will serve as preface to the essays that follow. These in no sense claim to be a complete treatment of the poet. They seek to distil the essence of his temper and grasp the secret of his style. They plead, first, that his genius be interpreted as consistently lyrical, in the sense that he could not write anything significant which was not essentially a quick mood expressed within narrow limits; and secondly, that his mood and its expression nevertheless require to be noticed and analysed with some care; he has his own idiom, and it is of a peculiar and subtle kind, emotionally direct, yet withal sophisticated and complex. I might phrase it that the critic's aim should be to capture the secret of his psychology rather than the story of his life, provided we remember that it is a poet's soul that we seek, and that such a soul is to be discovered, if anywhere at all, in his style.

Not that his power was any greater than that of other poets, or indeed as great as, for example, Virgil's. But it was more elusive, its results more transitory—how transitory I have sought to show in the last essay in this book, on *Lyric and Liberty*, where I have measured the space that we have to clear for his lyrics in the history of Latin poetry as a whole. His style is a fleeting thing, depending for its effect to a peculiar extent on the idiom and atmosphere of his day and generation. I am thinking for example of how he makes lyric out of light airy colloquialism, of how civilized his emotions are, how coloured and complicated by the values of a literary clique; of how, again, he can unexpectedly touch his verse with historical romance, how at other times he can confine its emotions within epigrammatic forms as exact as cross-word puzzles, and as intoxicating. To these imponderables of style and substance let us turn.

PESSIMUS POETA

IN striking contrast to Horace, who ended his three books of odes with the impressive boast that he had in them raised a monument more enduring than brass, Catullus offers a dedication for his own small book which reads like an apology. 'It was you' he writes to Cornelius Nepos, 'who used to think my bits of verse (*nugae*) amounted to something . . . so accept this book of mine, such as it is . . . ' (page 4). And again, in another fragmentary address to the reader (14b), he writes 'If perchance some of you will read these sorry pieces of mine (*ineptiae*), nor disdain to let your hands touch my pages. . . . ' The tone he thus chooses to adopt may be held the mark of native modesty; but it is also indirectly a reflection of official standards of Roman taste: it illustrates the curious position of Catullus in Latin literature. The poet's apology, we must remember, was not written for those more ambitious experiments of his which to-day seem so unsuccessful, nor is he apologizing mainly for his more casual lampoons and obscenities. He feels compelled to depreciate also those lyrics for which he is now gratefully remembered, the forty eleven-syllables, which include such favourites as the sparrow poems and *Lesbia's Kisses*, and the eleven iambics, including the *Salute to Sirmio* and the *Old Yacht* (*Phasellus ille, quem videtis, hospites*, no. 4).

Why was his most typical work a matter of apology rather than proud boast? There are three connected reasons which explain this. The first of them is indirectly revealed in a lyric written after meeting the man who became his bosom friend, the contemporary poet Calvus. 'It was only yesterday', he writes 'that we amused ourselves by using my tablets to improvise on, each of us scribbling bits of verse, improvising in one metre after another, keeping up the exchange while the jokes and the wine went round. At last I left and went home, fired by the memory of your charm and humour. . . .'[20] This little scene, laid in the last days of the republic, of two young men scribbling verse to each other across the dinner-table, deserves contemplation. It has something to say to us about the fateful history of Roman lyric, as ill-starred as the republic itself. The verse for which Catullus is now remembered, verse which official Roman taste subsequently decided was too frivolous to be taken seriously, was written in what might be termed conversational metres, which lent themselves to improvisation, such as is described in these very lines, themselves a sample of such occasional writing. The word 'improvise' has to be qualified carefully to be understood. Roman poetry as a whole borrowed its rhythms from the Greek, and Catullus and Calvus and other leaders of the contemporary movement in poetry were no exception to this rule. But Greek literature could provide two sorts of models. There were the grave hexameter and stately Alcaic and Sapphic metres in which Greek poetry first found perfect form. These were finally wedded to Latin through the efforts of Virgil and Horace. There were also the easier and lighter eleven-syllables and iambics which were so popular in the Alexandrian age. These were the rhythms which Catullus and his contemporaries most loved to manipulate. They found in them a medium close to the rhythm of ordinary conversation, and therefore easy to improvise in. Though, like all Latin metres modelled on the Greek, they were formally scanned by quantity, their beat coincided often enough with the accent of ordinary conversation to make them to this day the easiest ancient poetry to scan without intellectual effort. The Romans found them easy too, and this, because of the twist taken by Latin poetry and poetic taste, became their defect—a curious defect, one would think, in poetry, the mistress of pleasure, but the tale of this belongs to a later essay. Let it suffice for the moment to remember that the lyrics of Catullus, in the eyes of Roman posterity, could never be taken quite seriously, because they were written in apparently easy and spontaneous metres—because in fact they were lyrics.

Catullus was guilty not merely of occasional form, but also of occasional content, and this was true even when he deserted the lyric metres and wrote in the more difficult and artificial dactylic rhythms of his epigrams. These were short verses of from two to ten lines which he converted, as we shall see, into something not unlike lyrics themselves. The fact that these creations of his, whatever their metre, had to be filed and polished to reach perfection, does not alter the other fact, that they enshrined the passing mood and occasion. They became the vehicle of purely personal and temporary feeling, and this, measured by accepted standards of Roman poetry, became their second defect. Personal emotion, however sincerely felt, is fluctuating material for literary treatment; lyrically expressed, it refuses that discipline of intellect which produces either continuous epic or continuous elegy. It is as the wind blowing where it listeth. By modern canons, the mere expression of a mood of love or hate, despair or pity, if poetically successful becomes its own justification. But the Roman attitude was rather different. The younger Pliny, for example, apologizes for what he considers a mere hobby of his in the following terms: *His iocamur ludimus amamus dolemus querimur irascimur describimus aliquid modo pressius modo elatius atque ipsa varietate temptamus efficere ut alia aliis quaedam fortasse omnibus placeant.... Sed quid ego plura? nam longa praefatione vel excusare vel commendare ineptias ineptissimum est.*[21]

Love, grief, anger and despair—such is the register of human feeling which this Roman prig—and he was typical of the Roman temper in this respect—could treat as the object of light experiment, as literary frivolity. To reveal the complete heart was not enough, or rather, it was too much, and Catullus half-realized this himself. In a versified epistle of forty lines, otherwise of no great merit (68a: cf. note 6), he has one or two revealing passages of autobiography; this is one of them: 'From the time when I dropped the garments of boyhood, in the happy spring-time of my life, I have played at poetry to my heart's content; the goddess who mingles the bitter with the sweet knows me well.' The lyrics which he here describes and dismisses as 'play'[22] were, as his own language shows, those that had betrayed his most passionate moods. It is easy to see that in his secret heart such 'play' was taken as a far more serious and moving business than it ever became again in Latin literature. The passing mood of hope and love and grief and despair—it was all he had, the gift of his youth, a gift which the convention of his race and age compelled him to depreciate. Is it any wonder that Roman poetry produced no successor to Catullus, no singer—if we except the author of the anonymous *Pervigilium Veneris*—who could develop the free genius of lyric to its proper perfection?

Of all his emotions it was his love that crowned his verse. Yet this, by Roman standards, became a third reason why that verse had to be discounted. Any literary Roman could enjoy erotic verse, and might try his hand at writing it. The elegists indeed made a deliberate study of love, whether they dissected their own emotions in the manner of Propertius, or those of other people in the manner of Ovid. The originality of Catullus lay in making love completely tender and completely serious. This, whether or not it is to be explained as a Celtic aberration, was officially speaking a mistake in literary taste. The poet himself in his own life-time had to defend his 'thousands of kisses' against critics who interpreted them to mean effeminacy.[23] The truth is that the complete sincerity of his love for Lesbia, when expressed in occasional lyric, was a phenomenon too rare in

Roman literature to be properly estimated. What Roman taste could accommodate and understand was either the physical details, the obscene virtuosities of an Ovid or Martial, or else the erotic emotions and symptoms, the desires, tears, sighs, handled, one might say, systematically, in the manner of the elegists. Such verse could never be completely dignified, and was therefore not quite respectable, yet withal tolerated and enjoyed: it was either 'naughty' (*lascivus, parum pudicus, petulans*) or 'feminine' (*mollis, tener*). The literary attitude was not unlike the social treatment of prostitution. To quote Pliny again: *Si nonnulla tibi paulo petulantiora videbuntur, erit eruditionis tuae cogitare summos illos et gravissimos viros qui talia scripserunt non modo lascivia rerum sed ne verbis quidem nudis abstinuisse: quae nos refugimus, non quia severiores (unde enim?) sed quia timidiores sumus. Scimus alioqui huius opusculi illam esse verissimam legem quam Catullus expressit. . . .*[24]

Since these were the only categories of erotic poetry that Roman taste understood, into these the love lyrics of Catullus had to be fitted, and he himself adopted the idiom of his race in this matter, defending his personal morals by depreciating his own verse, in the famous apology

> *nam castum esse decet pium poetam*
> *ipsum, versiculos nihil necesse est,*
> *qui tum denique habent salem et leporem*
> *si sunt molliculi ac parum pudici.*

The context of these lines makes it clear that his description of verse both 'feminine' and 'naughty' is meant to include his passionate addresses to Lesbia[25] no less than his ribald invitations to a prostitute; the latter, indeed, might easily qualify as *parum pudici*, but not at all as *molliculi*. Catullus in fact defers, no doubt unconsciously, to contemporary taste in this description, as he had done also when he dismissed his lyric gift as juvenile 'play'. Posterity echoed these values.

'Naughty' is the epithet which to Ovid seemed appropriate to apply to his predecessor's most powerful poetry:

> *Sic sua lascivo cantata est saepe Catullo*
> *femina, cui falsum Lesbia nomen erat.*

True, he is apologising for his own naughtiness when he says this, but the limitations of Roman taste prevented him from seeing any incongruity between Catullus' more sincere lyrics of passionate feeling and his own erotic and heartless verse. Hence it became natural for all erotic poetry to be classed in Roman eyes as 'frivolous'. Ovid, again, proffering his own defence of personal morals, treats the moral and the frivolous as mutually exclusive categories

> *Vita verecunda est, musa iocosa mea.*[26]

Thus Catullus paid the price to Roman posterity of defying the unromantic Roman temper. He wrote love lyrics which his countrymen proved incompetent to classify and enjoy as modern taste may enjoy them. We have cleared a dignified space in literature for sexual passion; that is the difference. Virgil's treatment of the same theme illustrates from another side the same Roman limitations. With a temper equally sensitive, but much more cautious, his literary instincts seem early to have recognized the limits on feeling set by his audience. So he took care to treat love with a certain detachment, either playful or tragic. He can voice its emotions prettily, in such famous lines as these

> *Saepibus in nostris parvam te roscida mala—*
> *Dux ego vester eram—vidi cum matre legentem.*
> *Alter ab undecimo iam tum me acceperat annus,*
> *Iam fragiles poteram ab terra contingere ramos.*
> *Ut vidi, ut perii, ut me malus abstulit error!*[27]

But the bloom of tenderness on these lines remains a slight thing—a childish romance, not a grown man's passion. And when in later life he pitted the distracted Dido against the cautious disciplined Aeneas, love is still a *malus error*, and the outcome of the story an allegory of the fate which love suffered in Roman literature. Once only he allowed himself to transcend somewhat the Roman attitude, when he wrote the story of Orpheus and Eurydice which ends the fourth *Georgic*.

Thus because of the metrical form of his light lyrics, and the content which he put into both lyric and epigram, the place of Catullus in Roman literature remains for ever ambiguous. In consecrating his technique to the service of purely spontaneous feeling unmixed with reflection and concentrated on personal things, he crossed the accepted categories of Roman poetry without being able to create a new and completely valid one for himself.[28] He needed successors to establish what he had wrought, and none appeared. The elegiac love poets, Tibullus, Propertius, Ovid created only the illusion of such emotional expression. In fact their compositions, by virtue of their mere length and continuity, were compelled to make a study of love. Even Propertius is a professional love poet with his finger on the pulse, not a lover who writes poetry. As for Horace's odes, their inspiration, though of a different order, was equally professional (cf. page 178).

Yet the same qualities which half-disqualify Catullus as a serious Latin poet are precisely those which make him a lyrist, and, according to the judgment of a considerable body of modern opinion, the only authentic lyrist that Latin literature has produced. The paradox can be understood when certain limitations of the Roman temper are understood also. In a familiar passage of the *Aeneid* Virgil's countrymen are exhorted to leave the arts to other races and concentrate on their own appointed task of empire-building. The prescription was just. The poet was not pointing Rome to a new road, but merely exhorting her to follow one she had already taken. The results for Europe have been concrete—colonies, roads, law and language. To obtain government over Greek and barbarian, and keep it, required a genius for staying-power, compromise, authority and reserve, the supreme national virtue recognized by the Romans themselves as *gravitas*, a moral and mental discipline akin to Puritanism, which when dressed up in philosophy for the benefit of the intelligentsia became Stoicism. But they paid the Puritan price for this virtue, not only by frequent lapses into extremes of license, but, much more insidiously, by the suspicion and fear of ease and pleasure which fill the pages of Roman biographers, moralists and historians with innuendoes at the expense of the great. Any statesman, republican or imperial, whether a Sulla, Lucullus, Augustus or Tiberius, so rash as to flaunt the national *gravitas* by turning aside to wine, women and song becomes at once an object of gravest suspicion. We can see the thing in its extreme form in the innuendoes which the Stoic Seneca chose to record of Maecenas, the patron of letters, the friend and counsellor of Augustus, and one of the architects of the empire: 'His literary style was as loose as his morals'. 'He was less of a man than his two eunuchs were'.[29]

The national inhibitions revealed in such judgments imposed a special form of limitation on Roman literature which gradually destroyed it. The Greeks had wedded strong emotion to strict form in a happy marriage of equals. The Roman mind preferred to let form master emotion completely. Thus, borrowing the Greek patterns, it selected only what it considered the graver for serious treatment, and produced a schoolmasters' literature which because of its disciplined structure has remained to modern times an instrument of formal education second only to mathematics.

This is the technical way of putting it. But the limitations were not merely those of form. The oratorical periods of Cicero, the patriotism of Virgil, the moral sentiments of Horace, the thunderous invective of Juvenal, the sombre innuendoes of Tacitus, or the moral reflections of Seneca reflect in writing of different periods the defect of the Roman virtues. It is as though a Roman could never take up writing without taking up an attitude as well. Cicero's private letters or the humorous fantasies of Petronius reveal the Roman off-duty, and the effect is a refreshing shock, reminding us that *gravitas* in its literary form was always something of a pose. But how rarely is the revelation made, and how fatal this slight failure in sincerity, which killed Latin literature before its time, when the political structure had some centuries to live out! When we have taken the trouble to notice Cicero's ponderous public humour, have allowed Horace's skittishness to amuse us, and have savoured Martial's wittier epigrams, doubt remains whether one could laugh in Latin or make love in it, until we come upon the verses of Catullus.

Against the national temper and its limitations his poetry remains a protest. He pleads not only that an hour of love and laughter is worth a dozen Roman provinces, but in effect that the lyrical expression of the passing hour is worth a dozen histories and epics. For this Catullus stands convicted of both artistic and moral frivolity. He is not disciplined, he is fluctuating and extravagant and emotional and trivial, and because of these things no less than for his obscenity the schoolmaster finds him a poor discipline for wayward pupils.

He requires therefore to be read as the least Roman of the Romans, as we are accustomed to recognize them—creatures resembling the learned judge of Galsworthy, difficult to imagine as either dicing, dancing or in bed. His is not a strong sustained voice; he is juvenile and unequal. His work represents an attempt, unconscious and incomplete, to create a new genre of Roman poetry, but because he never cared to recognize the fact or to claim importance for it, his verse duly offers its apologies for insignificance. Yet he represents something precious, an inspiration which if caught and preserved might have saved Latin poetry from its swift decline. One is at liberty to imagine his departed spirit contemplating the poetic achievements of his successors with a certain irony, in a mood not unlike that in which during his own lifetime he saluted his grave contemporary Cicero. To the orator whose periods now form such apt models for Latin prose composition, he once wrote an ironic little note of thanks:

> *Disertissime Romuli nepotum,*
> *Quot sunt quotque fuere, Marce Tulli,*
> *Quotque post aliis erunt in annis,*
> *Gratias tibi maximas Catullus*
> *Agit pessimus omnium poeta,*
> *Tanto pessimus omnium poeta*
> *Quanto tu optimus omnium patronus.*[30]

Pessimus poeta let him remain. He can afford to be elbowed out of the hierarchy of Roman literature, for he scarcely belongs there.

BECAUSE the best of Catullus' verse reads so informally when set beside other Latin poetry, its style appears deceptively simple and plain. Attacking enemies, hailing friends, adoring and reviling his love, it conveys always an illusion of naïve spontaneity, which seems to constitute the protest of 'the worst poet in the world' against the formal spirit of his country's literature. Yet once having recognized his striking ability to express direct feeling in verse, we have to guard against the extreme view that here is a simple and naïve poet. Both his temper and his style are the reverse of naïve. His casual idiom is not the plain style of a Wordsworth, to which it has been compared. He presents the rare spectacle of a character highly complicated, but yet spontaneous, expressing itself in an idiom which has the direct simplicity of conversation, yet is completely sophisticated.

Consider for example the manner of his *Salutation to Sirmio*, his country home and his jewel. On the one hand he can afford to let himself go, expressing naïve emotion with unaffected simplicity. Sirmio, he feels, is so lovely, and how glad he is to look on it again, how grateful to drop his burden and sink upon the pillow of his dreams. These parts of the poem are in truth a plain expression of simple emotion. But the general setting is otherwise; in the half-humorous address to the half-island, the conceit by which Neptune is duplicated, one for fresh water one for salt, the touch of self-depreciation as he describes his bewildered pleasure, and the fantasy which imagines laughter lurking in the place —these things are both emotionally unaffected and yet in their expression the essence of affectation.

This mood of his, though it gives his verse a flavour shared by no other Latin poet, is very difficult to define or describe. To call it sophistication would imply that it was a mere convention superimposed upon the surface of his deeper emotions, as though he had a way of expressing himself which had nothing to do with what he felt. But the surface of him is part of the substance, his style expresses his whole character, his sophistication (we may say) was sincere because his emotions themselves, though powerful, were also sophisticated.

This virtue in him could be summed up most adequately as his urban consciousness, especially when we remember the affinities of 'urban' with 'urbane', though 'urbane' as used to-day by no means describes all the qualities of the *urbanus*. Catullus was *par excellence* an urban poet, and first of all in a quite literal sense. We know from his own verse that he soon left his native haunts for Rome. But then, so did most Roman writers at some time in their lives, if they had not been lucky enough to be born there; they found it congenial to move to the metropolis and there find patrons, colleagues, critics and a public. In Rome accordingly we find Catullus, moving in political and literary society, making friends and enemies. This all seems very proper and natural, and not very significant, especially when we notice also that like Horace he had his little suburban farm and like Virgil retained affection for his Cisalpine country home. However, the matter wears a different complexion in the light of a short statement—it is really a confession—which occurs in that same disjointed but revealing epistle in which were described the bitter-sweet experiences of his spring-time. I cannot, he says, write here at Verona: 'Rome is the place where I live, to Rome I ever return; there do my years bear their fruit'[31]. These emphatic words, like his previous references to his early poetry, are in the nature of a self-revelation. They describe not a convenient and agreeable postal address, but a source of inspiration. He, like Socrates, found that only the city and the busy haunts of men could inspire or instruct him.

He does not philosophize about this, for he was no philosopher; he accepts the city unconsciously, and in this is quite unlike the run of Latin poets. Lucretius, Virgil, Horace and Juvenal probably represent the merit and variety of Latin poetry as well as any four that could be chosen. All of them betray urban weariness; they distrust the city and its ways; not in crowded streets and salons is mental health and peace to be found. The country and country simplicity is for them the essential avenue of escape. But Catullus as he returns to Sirmio does not think of representing himself as the town gentleman retiring to rural simplicity. The burden which his mind drops is the fatigue of foreign travel, not urban conventions and conversation. In what appears to be a rustic poem he does not think it necessary to speak with the rusticity of Burns or worship nature in the Wordsworthian manner.

The Roman puritanism with which he had so little in common always professed to recoil from the complications of city life. We have grown so used to animadversions on the subject uttered by Roman writers that we have come to accept the moral preference for rural simplicity as right and proper on their part. When Horace sighs for his Sabine farm, Virgil exclaims on the happiness of the farmer's life, and Lucretius reproaches the character of the urban idler, we think we are meeting a healthy attitude. It too rarely occurs to us that this attitude of escape was barren, that it quite missed the Greek genius which accepted urban civilization and sought to refine it and interpret its goals, that since urban life is the essential nourishment of a civilization, rejection of its values by these writers was insincere, and menaced their integrity. Catullus by contrast is integral; he is not frustrated by the desire to escape; the city to him means creative freedom, not a prison. He would have understood the Marxists who summon our civilization to reject the stupid isolation of rural life.[32]

The results for his poetry were important. He was not enough of a philosopher to generalize about the urban consciousness. His tastes were not catholic. But he does express the spirit and essence of 'society' set within inverted commas, that privileged fraction of urban civilization which apparently, to judge from our use of the word, we still feel to represent the quintessence of urban culture. Within this group he moved, breathing the one atmosphere which could inspire him and kindle his verse.

That circle of fashion in Rome in the last century of the era was at once narrow and intense. The like of it the city never saw again, compounded of quite the same proportions of learning and love, snobbery and sympathy, literature and politics. Many causes contributed these ingredients. Politically, the upper class were still free; culturally, they had just drunk the intoxicating wine of Greek literature; morally they were emancipated through the emancipation of upper-class women. The general result seems to have been that 'society' became for a brief period a creative group, leisured but not idle, privileged but also self-critical, capable of stimulating the songs of poets and of tolerating their lampoons. Around its dinner-tables men compared the arts of Greece and planned the politics of Rome. Statesmen and business men who had received the new Greek education found themselves in the midst of practical affairs not immune to philosophy and poetry. We do not catch in Catullus any direct echo of their more serious thoughts and important intrigues. The associations which the poet's temperament found congenial were those kindled in the narrow but intense realm of friendship and love. Fragments of laughter, personal reminiscences, fashionable colloquialisms drift down two thousand years to us in his verse.

He gives no formula for this urban consciousness; to formulate it might destroy it, since its essence is a kind of tacit agreement between a certain number of people to speak and behave in a certain manner. It implies first an attitude and style of behaviour, and second a style of expression, a manner of speech. As to the first, it makes the supreme virtues those which in conventional morality are reduced to matters of taste or accident of character. Personal nicety, suitable to the lover and mistress; personal loyalty, which preserves the intimacies of friendship unspoiled and does not betray them; a sensitive imagination capable of dealing with the subtleties alike of personal relationships and literary taste. Such are some of the unconscious standards of the Catullan ideal, to be illustrated from his own verse.

But while such standards were unconscious and unwritten, the style of expression that went with them became very conscious. *Urbanitas* as it is mentioned in Catullus[33] therefore refers particularly to that capacity which can use the proper idiom. Twice he makes a literary judgment in terms which imply a wide gulf between the urban and rural, the ways of the city and the dull isolation of the peasant, as if 'urbanity' were the criterion of good poetic diction and style. Once he asks the reader to contemplate Suffenus, who displays all the outward symptoms of an *urbanus*, but is unwise enough to take to verse writing, with disastrous results, being at once revealed as a 'clodhopper', and again, the chronicles composed by Volusius are mere sheets of toilet paper, they 'reek of the country'.[34] In this sharp literary antithesis we catch the whole mood of that small and precious circle in which he lived, a circle founded precariously on the labour of the countless lives of the peasantry, created swiftly in the swift rise of Latin prosperity and living uneasily under the shadow of coming revolution, keenly conscious of itself, its privileges, its difference, its unique flavour of cultivated civilization.

What was this urban idiom, mastery of which was so important, and absence so fatal? A large part of it was a habit of colloquialism. But this did not mean slang; it was a colloquialism of the intelligentsia, a manipulation of language which gave it extra and allusive power, yet made it seem fragile and frivolous. Quintilian, in days when this brilliance had left Roman society, produced a ponderous but adequate formula for it: *Nam et urbanitas dicitur, qua quidem significari video sermonem praeferentem in verbis et sono et usu proprium quendam gustum urbis, et sumptam ex conversatione doctorum tacitam eruditionem, denique cui contraria sit rusticitas.*[35] This sentence may be cited with justice to explain one of the secrets of Catullus' style. Not only does it point to the fact that his 'urbanity' is a matter of idiom (*sono et usu*) cultivated in self-conscious opposition to the ways of the country, but in order to describe urbanity's content it selects two significant words—*tacitam eruditionem*. Here indeed is the secret to be found—in an intellectualism, not avowed and advertized as it is by the professional men of intellect, the professors and philosophers, but disguised, deprecated, concealed (*tacitam*), handled casually and colloquially (*sumptam ex conversatione*), an attitude the very antithesis of learning and pedantry, an attitude which regarded a dull piece of writing as the worst crime in the world.[36] 'O saeclum insapiens et infacetum!' he cries (page 22) of a generation insensitive even to the personal charms of his Lesbia. The truly wise (*sapiens*) had to master more than book-learning to conform to his standard; they that failed to attain were not merely 'unwise', they were 'without taste'.

This is the style of Catullus; his simple directness is partly an illusion; he speaks the idiom of cultivated colloquialism, that idiom of which he is thinking when he describes the *urbanus* as also *venustus* and *dicax*. Cicero with more elegance but less precision than Quintilian was trying to describe the same quality when he referred to Lysias, the Greek orator, father of 'Atticism', as '*subtilis, elegans, venustissimus, politissimus.*'[37] The subtle charm that links Lysias with Catullus is the cultivated use of conversational idiom. *Dicax* does not

mean the mere ability to handle words. Some 'good conver-
sationalists' would merely have amused the poet. It was the
ability to handle them allusively, and one might almost add
poetically, only this suggests something too flowery and
pretentious. Catullus' brand of verse is lyric, but it is colloquial and careless lyric. Its phrasing often conveys richer
meaning, more subtle allusion, than the non-urbanus can
manage. But the thing must be done lightly, ironically,
deprecatingly, with a slight twist. He does not always write
so; a few of his epigrams are as bare as prose (e.g. pp. 30, 58.)
But he writes like that oftener than we are inclined to notice.

So much by way of general warning and preparation for
those who desire to taste the full flavour of this poet. The
essays which follow, as they seek to analyse various aspects
of the Catullan temper, and particularly his *venustas*, will also
provide concrete illustrations of this *urbanitas* from his verse.
To conceal affection in a diminutive, to call his friends
opprobrious names or address them as *bellus* and *venustus*
('You dear creature'), to convey some allusion of history or
mythology in a casual phrase, while deriding the finicking
pedantries of a man like Caesar ('acquiring a little culture on
the sofa'[38])—these are some of its effects. A collection of
grammatical colloquialisms[39] fails to convey the effect of
this conversational yet cultivated manner, because the
manner relies on using non-colloquial words in a slightly
colloquial context: *Quaeris quot mihi basiationes Tuae Lesbia
sint satis superque* (page 16). The abstract form of the noun
is a mannerism, with a caress in it. *Hesterno, Licini, die otiosi
Multum lusimus in meis tabellis Ut convenerat esse delicatos.* (no
50). The combination of *convenerat* and *delicatos* is untranslatable; it conveys the sense of an unwritten compact which
only the initiated could understand.

Since the world of scholarship is largely immune to this
manner, it can make very little of the Catullan charm, which
to the serious-minded will pass unnoticed, or else be mis-

interpreted as either vulgarity or Wordsworthian plainness of diction. Yet Catullus is separated by many leagues from the Wordsworthian manner, as from the Wordsworthian mind. In English letters, Wilde offers a closer parallel—the same sophistication, the same extravagance, the same epigrammatic intellect, the same emotional sincerity lapsing into moral license, the same paradoxical blend of lyric and mannerism. And this elusive compound was wedded also to an artistic creed. The neoterics of Catullus' circle, (discussed below in the essay on *Lyric and Liberty*) had many things in common with the pre-Raphaelites of Victorian England.

'Culture' is a poor label for this compound; it had the unconscious ease of French civilization, not the studied and laborious learning of Germany. 'Good God!' says Catullus of the world-history compiled by his friend Nepos, 'What learned and laboured volumes!' The comment is not merely personal; it reflects the values of his literary set; and reminds us how misleading can be the epithet 'scholar' which posterity applied to the poet. Of this also I shall speak again. All Roman litterateurs were stylists in their careful way, but with a difference. Perhaps if we think of what Cicero meant by *humanitas*, and compare with it what Catullus meant by *venustas*, we can realize the difference. Roman 'humanism' had its merits, but it remained always slightly pompous. It could never of itself have kindled the Italian renaissance without the extra touch of Italian extravagance and subtlety of imagination, qualities anticipated by Catullus alone of the Latin succession.

HOMO VENUSTUS

THE greater poets not infrequently embody elements of their human ideal in some notable character, an Odysseus, an Aeneas, a Prometheus, a Satan. Catullus was incapable of any such creation. Nevertheless, his verse conveys a type, a standard, a design for living which becomes almost the spirit of his poetry. *Homo disertus, venustus, bellus, facetus, urbanus*—such is the creature that lurks in the lines of his verse, the ideal, compounded of wit and charm, love and loyalty, humour and extravagance, lettered, civilized, sensitive, to which he gave allegiance. Can the ingredients be analysed? The answer may not seem intrinsically very important, for these days of social change, when fascism and communism clash over Europe, and men restlessly demand justice and bread, are too earnest, alas, to leave much room even in poetry for the charming and frivolous hour, the bloom on the peach, the crown of civilization. We are far too conscious that our civilization is at present being rebuilt to contemplate what its crown may be. Yet without these things there is no meaning in Catullus' verse; its substance is that of the leisured hour—*ut convenerat esse delicatos*—its flavour a peculiar spice of civilized manners, and to recapture it, we have to notice some of the ingredients, even at the risk of committing that same pedantry which the completely civilized are so careful to avoid.

(i) His Elegance

It was, for example, the soul of wit, an essence required even in love. Quintia had a good figure, good looks—and yet, what a lump of a girl, what a pudding, unflavoured by any spice of subtlety! How different was the quick charm of his own Lesbia. With wit, moreover, must go breeding and discretion, that ready sense which knows how to pronounce correctly, to avoid the pitfalls of the aspirate, how to behave at a party. These things are naturally taken for granted: only their absence is noticed. There was Arrius, who could not get the "h" stuck on the right word, and Egnatius, who suffered from a nervous grin which appeared on all the wrong occasions.[40] This, poor fellow, was the ultimate error—one of taste, and the poet damns such inelegant behaviour for ever in a line whose own verbal elegance is complete—*nam risu inepto res ineptior nulla est*. Then there was Asinius, that social failure, who thought it would look Bohemian at parties if he carried off valuable table linen for souvenirs. It is the sordid gracelessness of the thing, rather than dishonesty, which affects the poet—

> *fugit te, inepte;*
> *quamvis sordida res et invenusta est.*

Such social incompetence requires the guidance of a younger but better-bred brother—*disertus puer*—who knows what is done and not done, what is funny and what isn't.[41] Nor are the requirements of good taste limited by such matters of social behaviour. They invade love's realm, and colour love's vocabulary. Varus takes him to meet his girl—'a charming dainty little thing, as I noticed directly I met her.' But Flavius has picked up somebody about whom he would apparently rather not tell—Is his treasure not so 'dainty', not so 'elegant' as she might be?[42] So firm is the grip of fashion that even the deepest emotion, and the bitterest, if it is vain, can be viewed simply as a lapse in taste:

> Poor Catullus, you should stop being clumsy: (*desinas ineptire*)
> Let what is fled be as the dead (page 52)

No wonder that a poet whose standards of behaviour were so exacting should have written verse itself so charming, deft, as daintily clever as Humbert Wolfe's—'Who's to receive this dainty little volume?' This, the first line of his dedication, does not refer merely to the results of the binder's art; it notices that quality in his verse which was perhaps its most conscious and studied attribute. For the daintiness, the lightness, as it appears, of such verses as *Lesbia's Tears*, *Lesbia's Kisses*, *Lesbia's Question*, is the result of a consummate craftsmanship in form, fitted to the taste of a period which regarded the essence of style as elegance. 'I would like to cry the tale of your love to the heavens' he tells Flavius; but the verse in which he is to tell this loud tale must be 'elegant'.[43]

(ii) His Gusto

But wit and dexterity and good taste, while they belong to lyric, are not the essence of it. They would have made Catullus into a Martial but not into a poet. Indeed, such qualities are so close to snobbery that they can be dangerous to lyric: the snob cannot sing, and Catullus can, even in epigram. How does he do it? The answer can be expressed in part by saying that to his wit was added gusto; as he himself says to Fabullus, proffering him a gay invitation to dinner—'Bring wine and wit, and lots of laughter too.'[44] His poetry may occasionally be poor stuff, but, except in one or two experimental studies, it is never inhibited. This fact is partly a tribute to his period. In a cultivated age, the critic always lurks at the elbow of the artist, cramping his emotions and making him too self-conscious, for he is always thinking how his friends or the reviewers or posterity will read his stuff. But in Ciceronian and republican Rome, with political liberty still preserved, and a new literature just in process of flowering, its creators, even as they put behind them the archaic and ponderous poetry of Ennius and his school, felt the emotional release proper to an experimental period. They were not all lucky enough to be able to express this release with genius, but Catullus was their prototype, saved by a certain exuberance, a quality frequently described in his verse 'amid the laughter and the wine'.[45] '*Iucundus*'— 'you funny one'—is among his favourite epithets, and 'to have fun' one of the most precious of all activities. His best friend Calvus and his darling Lesbia were both fond of fun, she with her pet bird, he with his improvised verse; this was one of the things that made him love them in the days of his own 'laughing youth', as he called it.[46] There is an emotional spontaneity here, urbane yet direct, to which only the single-hearted have the secret; it prefigured a virtue alien to the Roman pose, at least in literature. It would not occur to graver writers to catch the note of laughter in the word 'home', as Catullus did; Horace could unbend, but not quite in that boyish way; there is too much of the golden mean about him, even in his banter.

Such gusto created his lampoons, and released the obscenities which spoil many of them for modern taste. Let it be admitted that his own taste sometimes fumbled. He ran the risks which a strong self-assured nature must often take. It has been well suggested that the more repellent were written in the morbid mood of his last two years, with brother dead and Lesbia lost and his own life already burning out. His most effective attacks are written in a kind of extravagance which carries them along, yet the modern misses the effect, because he who translates a dead tongue translates it with a careful attention the reverse of extravagant, and reads considered meaning into uproarious slang and drastic innuendoes.[47]

(iii) His Irony

But the matter for Catullus did not end in mere uproariousness. Time and again the poet praises what he calls *facetiae*, of which our 'facetiousness' is a derivative but by no means a synonym. He saw the quality in Calvus, and describes how it 'inflamed' him. The young Pollio had also mastered its secret; its presence in him was one of the hall-marks of that good sense so lamentably lacking in his brother. In both these instances *facetiae* is linked with *lepores*, meaning 'charm'. The lack of it—*infacetiae*—damned the dull ponderous poetic chronicle of his contemporary Volusius and stamped it as a 'rural' production.[48] Used in these contexts, the word becomes not merely 'humour' but 'a sense of humour' and even 'a sense of proportion'—'*O saeclum insapiens et infacetum*' he cries of a generation so crass as to miss Lesbia's charm (page 22). A civilized attitude this, half frivolous, half ironic, an attitude of his period and circle, which considered it good form to refuse to take serious matters too seriously. He lived in one of those brief crucial periods when the uninhibited gusto of earlier and ruder times could fuse with the self-critical temper of an urban culture. Thus a friend's love-affair is dignified by no greater title than 'an aberration', and even his own dextrous verses receive smiling apology in the same terms.[49]

What I have so far described—if my interpretation of *facetiae* and its implications is correct—is largely a matter of good form—rather like the convention which compels the English athlete to conceal his blue. However that may be, there is in Catullus very assuredly also a personal and deeper trait, a fundamentally ironic attitude to the world at large and to himself. It lurks half-concealed behind the wit and boisterousness, and those that miss it miss half his flavour. For ten who refuse to take the world seriously, there is usually found only one who does not take himself too seriously, but Catullus is a poet in that precious minority, which is the more surprising in a poet of love. He offers that rarest of all combinations, passion and humility; he has Shelley's intensity without Shelley's egoism, a fact strikingly illustrated in this, that the sole piece of moralizing in his lyrics is a testimonial to that virtue which can 'see ourselves as others see us'.[50] This temper of self-criticism, always slight, never over-stressed, emerges imperceptibly over and over again. Sestius' poetry is poor stuff, but after all Catullus has only himself to blame if he reads it. It is very embarrassing to be pestered by a pert girl for the loan of a carriage he has not got; but if he will boast of imaginary possessions, what else is to be expected?[51] There is something in this attitude close to the naïveté of children. He confesses ruefully, for example, that while the best people go to Tibur for a holiday (Horace later took care to underline the fact that he went there himself!) his own country-retreat is uneasily perched on the very edge of the fashionable and expensive district, and maybe should not be counted in it at all. He admits to being sensitive on the point, having the capacity to be hurt by a sneer.[52] He writes his little dedication (p. 4) for some of his verses, deprecating their standing and importance, and addresses the dedication to Cornelius Nepos the impressive historian, the only authority who had considered them worth noticing.

Minds that are self-critical in this way are often accused of false modesty, as though they were guilty of inverted boasting. But the accusation misses the mark, for it fails to notice that this deprecating sort of humour is exercised at the expense not merely of oneself but of things in general, putting the world in perspective, though not a perspective which serious and important people would always approve. In his dedication he refuses to be serious about his own occasional verse, but he cannot be completely serious about Nepos' terrific volumes either—a perfect illustration of this double irony. He does not often use it as a weapon, though once, in the address to Cicero (page 96), expressing thanks 'from the world's worst poet, to the world's best . . . lawyer,' its edge is keen. Usually it becomes that gentle humour with which for example he contemplates his Sirmio—an island, no not quite, only half a one perhaps (page 8). Or again, Lesbia's sparrow has died, and the enormous event is announced in a poem which celebrates the poor bird's virtues, pictures it hopping down the road to Hades, and is roused to an ironic outburst against death the destroyer—of even such a pretty little thing as a bird. But what is the inspiration of the whole piece, and its climax? Not the bird or its doom. The unlucky little victim indeed shares in the general condemnation, for provoking . . . a few tears glistening in his lady's eye! So is the subject of the verse finally relegated to its proper importance: the sense of proportion is preserved, and the poem saved from that slight error of exaggeration which might have made it ludicrous (page 20). We are not asked to become too pathetic over the fate of a canary bird; indeed, it is difficult to find an adjective appropriate to his attitude, for it is just too slight and too sophisticated to be either wistful or bitter. Though it helps to suggest to him the diminutives of which he is so fond, he uses them till they become little more than a pretty convention—as in the famous *turgiduli rubent ocelli*. It certainly inspires his use of neuter genders and indefinites, urban colloquialisms these, which as it were slightly reduce the status of their subject, and thus temper even affection and pathos with irony—

> *Quare habe tibi quidquid hoc libelli*
> *Qualecunque* (page 4)
> > or
> *Lugete, O Veneres Cupidinesque*
> *Et quantum est hominum venustiorum* (page 20)
> > or
> *O quantum est hominum beatiorum*
> *Quid me laetius est beatiusve* (9. 10–11)

Once only his ironic mood becomes strong and sorrowful, in the last supreme utterance of his shattered love. 'She need not cast another glance at my affection, for she was frail, and it fell and died like a flower at the edge of the field, after the passing plough has touched it' (page 66). His love had been

cut off, but after all it was only a wildflower blooming unbidden by the spare space in the hedge, not important
enough to arrest the severe course of events. Self-irony has
never been used with more power or pathos.

Such might be called irony in the Socratic sense, springing
always from an undercurrent of feeling that man with all his
wisdom is worth very little—his brief day ends: (*Nobis
cum semel occidit brevis lux, Nox est perpetua una dormienda*).
The Hebrew poet however who cried 'What is man, that
thou art mindful of him?' was not ironical. He found refuge
from the thought in aspiration; the ironical man finds it in a
smile and a shrug of the shoulders. That is why the rustic in
particular is so *infacetus*, as Catullus twice[53] observes. He is
humourless because he has no time to contemplate his own
lack of importance: he lacks irony. Similarly Socrates in the
course of his defence, when for once he abandons his ironic
vein to catalogue a few of his merits, feels obliged to
apologize for 'this piece of rusticity'.[54] The usage reminds us
that while pre-urban society can achieve a Homeric gusto
which is often lost later, only the urban temper can manage
self-criticism. Catullus was sure enough of himself to be able
to depreciate himself, a capacity which again demonstrated
his entire lack of provincialism. He had not that slight
inferiority complex, born of an inferior station in life, which
Horace and Virgil and Juvenal, the three powerful poets of
imperial Rome, found it so necessary to correct in themselves:

> *Lesbius est pulcher—Quid ni, quem Lesbia malit
> Quam te cum tota gente, Catulle, tua?*[55]

Here in his fierce resentment, when he drops all deprecation
and speaks with the arrogance of the gently-born, he reveals
how fundamental was that careless pride and assurance
which could normally afford to forget itself in order to
charm.

(iv) His Affection

Such are some of the ingredients of the Catullan ideal. But the chief of them we have yet to consider, the capacity to love. The ancient philosophers could discover in our transitory life only two things which were in themselves valuable, and needed no further end to justify them. One was human affection, the other the contemplation of truth. If Catullus had ever cared to rationalize his life's purposes, he would have acknowledged allegiance to the first of these. This it was that governed the values even of his poetry, and yet, without an extra effort of sympathy, our modern mood will miss it. We miss it because we think we have seen it. Catullus we recognize as what we call a 'love poet', meaning by this that he was inspired by an exclusive sexual desire for a woman to write a few passionate verses about her. We notice also that he often uses the language of tenderness and affection in other contexts which we presume are irrelevant to his passion, and that his verses include the tale of various sexual adventures and an affection for a boy which we dismiss as emotionally frivolous. This accomplished, we think we have comprehended the range of our 'love poet'.

To include all forms of human affection in one synthesis has not been attempted since the days of Plato. The convention of our civilization continues to ignore the teaching of psychology by relegating sexual desire to one compartment and all other forms of enthusiasm and affection to another. Sexual feeling is treated as *sui generis*, and pseudo-romanticism would even isolate romantic love as something quite apart from the rest of our sexual symptoms. If therefore it manifests itself in exclusive possession and jealousy, if its emotional field is sharply separated from other interests and relationships, that is taken to be natural and inevitable even by those that suppose themselves emancipated. The traditions and instincts of sexual property and possession, maintained through thousands of years, die very hard.

At any rate, Catullus cannot be understood as he deserves within these categories. I am not thinking merely of the fact that his mistress was another man's wife, though the fact, in the circumstances of his age, does not affect the validity of his love. He cannot be understood unless we realize that at the root of all his emotional attitudes lay a capacity for affection and an absorption in personal relationships with men and women, which issued in friendship, in sexual love, and in his love of poetry alike—distinctions these, but without a basic emotional difference; they were all alike *exciting* to him. Thus his verse continually betrays a sort of enthusiasm of affection for his friends. Calvus or Veranius could inspire him to expressions not elsewhere found in similar contexts in Latin literature: 'I tossed in frenzy on my bed all night, longing for the dawn which would bring us together again'; and to Veranius 'How I will kiss your happy face, and your eyes'.[56] This kind of sympathy can stretch itself to the point where it embraces the friend's friend, or even his mistress. Varus and Caecilius had other loves, but this very fact drew him to them: 'My dear Varus wanted me to meet his own dear one, so he took me off . . .'; and again 'O paper, take a message to Caecilius, poet of love, and my dear companion.'[57] This last example shows how his love of persons and poetry commingled. Literature was an activity for him like a personal relationship, and had the same exciting quality. The two activities indeed depended on each other, for poetic composition waited on personal intimacy to inspire it. The same charm, the same taste, were the touchstones of friendship, of poetry and of love. Thus we see him falling in love with Calvus while the pair of them scribble verses to each other. If Calvus had not been able to share his mental excitement he would not have gone down to history as Catullus' companion. The two men shared a similar romanticism toward sexual relations, as witnesses the elegy which Calvus wrote on his dead wife. And when Catullus in turn wrote his grave and pathetic epigram (page 36) to Calvus to comfort him, not only does affection for his friend touch his thought of the friend's wife with an imaginative sympathy, but he thinks too of the elegy which Calvus had created. When he says 'She may still rejoice in your love' he may very well be referring to that love's poetic expression, the elegy which she can perhaps hear even in death. Such an allusion would be in complete keeping with his faculty of blending friendship and poetry as kindred enthusiasms.

When friendship grows unhappy, it makes him disclose its inner values; he reveals the fact that for him affection and love are almost a personal religion. 'O Alfenus, you have forgotten all; you have betrayed companions that were united in soul'. 'I believed in you, Rufus—oh so vainly, so foolishly; nay, rather, say at cost of great woe'.[58] Loyalty, and sincerity, and complete surrender in affection—this is the creed by which he lives. Therefore in friendship he finds moral purpose, and when friendship is over, its most poignant memory is the 'benefits forgot', which do nothing to heal the loss, but, as he realized with sure insight, protest for ever against it—'It means nothing to have rendered a service—nay, more, the memory of it turns even to bitterness; we wish it had never been'.[59] Therefore also the quality of friendship alone could move him to invoke religion and the gods—'Can the disloyalties of them that betray man find favour in heaven's sight?'—'You can forget, but the gods remember.' *Pietas*, the most solemn of the virtues, is for him simply unswerving fidelity and generosity in personal relationships. 'Think no more' he tells himself in one bitter mood, 'think no more to try to serve men and earn their gratitude; hope no more that any man can be made loyal and true (*pium*).'[60]

The three laments for broken friendship from which these latter quotations are taken (nos. 30, 73 and 77 in the standard editions) are all powerful and revealing, but of all his affections, that for his brother inspired his most moving verse—

> *Quandoquidem fortuna mihi tete abstulit ipsum—*
> *Heu miser indigne frater adempte mihi.*

Death was 'unworthy', it violated all human canons, because it alone could permanently defeat the virtue of affection—the only virtue he believed in. Three times[61] in his versified epistles he returns to this irrevocable loss, and twice echoes these words. Posterity, though it did not bestow any particular notice on this fraternal link—in itself fairly uncommon—did remember that this David had his Jonathan, and in Calvus had found a bond of affection and of poetry—

> *Obvius huic venias hedera iuvenalia cinctus*
> *Tempora cum Calvo, docte Catulle, tuo.*[62]

It was rare insight in Ovid thus to link literary fame with literary friendship.

(v) The Language of Love

In his love for Lesbia all this religion of personal affection crystallized, and without it his love's expression cannot be understood. Hungry desire, passionate embrace, torturing jealousy—his verse has all these, the common attributes of Aphrodite Pandemos, but it also has something more, a touch of the ideal. Thus inspired, he can express an almost impersonal surrender, a joy in giving without return—

> *Nulla fides ullo fuit umquam in foedere tanta*
> *Quanta in amore tuo ex parte reperta mea est* (page 26)

and again the protective affection of a father—

> *Dilexi tum te non tantum ut vulgus amicam*
> *Sed pater ut gnatos diligit et generos* (page 56)

and again the supreme bitterness of benefits forgot—

> *Si qua recordanti benefacta priora voluptas*
> *Est homini, cum se cogitat esse pium . . .* (page 60)

till at the end, as the edifice of love crumbles, he is moved to open confession that such affection was his personal religion, the faith by which he lived—

O di, reddite mi hoc pro pietate mea. (page 62)

Pietas for Virgil's Aeneas meant the desertion of Dido in the cause of country; for Catullus it meant the world well lost for Lesbia. The contrast illustrates the deep division in temper which separates him from the official literature of Rome. Dido stands in Latin literature as the classic embodiment of passionate love, yet in the supreme crisis of her affection she remains faithful to the Roman type and reveals its limitations—

> At least, if but a child were born
> Of me to thee, ere thou wert gone,
> At very least, a little son
> Still to recall thy face to me . . . [63]

Many generations have felt the beauty and pathos of the passage. Yet she speaks as a Roman matron, a potential mother, not as a mistress. Only Catullus was capable of thinking of a woman not as a means to an end, but as worth everything in herself.

There are, it is true, other aspects of his erotic verse which to the psychoanalyst would seem less romantic than morbid. Jealousy could whip him up to the point of attacking his rivals in love with anatomical obscenity. This however was the fashion of the times, and he follows it with equal vigour in attacking political enemies and in fact anyone he does not happen to like. His character is revealed more intimately in the fact that even to friends like Calvus and Veranius he used the language of a lover. As for the boy Juventius, the subject of six verses, he treats him both as his beloved and his son, though this relationship again followed contemporary fashion. Now, to place the label homosexual on these expressions of feeling is totally misleading. The modern man uses the term to explain a set of instincts which are incapable of normal hetero-sexual expression. This explanation is obviously irrelevant to the case of a poet of such instincts as his. But it is true to say that there was in him a strong dash of the feminine, as indeed there is in all well-rounded and fully-matured natures, for it is an ingredient which has nothing to do with effeminacy. This bi-sexualism indeed on the part of both men and women is the psychological secret of that romanticism which since the passing of antiquity has been imported into the relation between the sexes; the man has grown more tender and the woman more protective—a symptom, this, that civilization is slowly coming of age. Catullus united a very full emotional nature with an unusual capacity for expressing it in poetry. Each increased the other, and as a result he far outstripped the emotional register of his race and period.[64]

This explains a remarkable thing about him—his capacity for identifying Lesbia with himself. For example, in the *Epistle to Allius* (page 39), looking back over his love's early days, and overcome by his yearning for her, in imagination he sees himself as she might be—as woman and wife—just as he sees her as he is himself—loving, faithful and patient. This is the secret of the twin poetic images of Laodamia and Juno as he used them in that poem. The tale of Laodamia forms an episode which has puzzled commentators, for it is the tale of a wife completely devoted to her husband as Lesbia never was to him—he confesses it in the same poem. The truth is that he has created her in the image of his own heart, because he cannot help it, and Laodamia is the embodiment of this illusion, half Lesbia, and half himself. Like Lesbia, she was a lovely and famous woman; like himself, she loved too well and found her love frustrated—

> *Coniugis ante coacta novi dimittere collum*
> *Quam veniens una atque altera rursus hiems*

> *Noctibus in longis avidum saturasset amorem,*
> *Posset ut abrupto vivere coniugio.* (page 42).

So Lesbia after all was not really like her: the image remains an illusion—

> *Aut nihil aut paulo cui tum concedere digna*
> *Lux mea se nostrum contulit in gremium*—(page 44)

the stumbling apologetic comparison is very pitiful. Later in the poem, when he reminds himself of Lesbia's frailties, the image that rises before his eyes is that of Juno, goddess and queen as was Lesbia (even Cicero admits as much, likening her to Hera), but also the wife faithful and patient, tolerant of Jove's infidelities as he was resolved to be of hers. And yet, he goes on to remind himself, he had as a matter of fact no right at all to call her wife, or lend her either protection or patience. She was only a love 'stolen from husband's bed', and the thought inspires one of the poem's most poignant passages (page 45).

As he can thus endow her with his own absorbing passion, so conversely he can imagine for her a destitution which is really his own. 'Ah', he cries, when he is trying to resolve to leave her, 'Yours will be the heartache, the loss'.

> *At tu dolebis, cum rogaberis nulla;*
> *Scelesta, vae te! quae tibi manet vita* . . . (page 52).

In this fashion he makes his loss hers. If therefore as we read his love-verses we are deceived into thinking that we have grasped Lesbia's image, this is a tribute to the feminine in him, which enabled him so to identify himself with her. He had a trick of seeing her not as she was, wayward, fickle, perhaps heartless and shallow, but as the substance of his own emotions; a supreme victory this, for love to wring from defeat.

His senses pervert themselves only when they are frustrated. He notices face and feet and figure in Lesbia's rivals with cruel attention, because they are aesthetic failures, and

their personages disintegrate (pages 22, 24). When betrayal had made him morbid, he spoke once of Lesbia's lovers
caught in her catholic embrace and crushed (page 66), and
in another verse (p. 64), torturing his imagination with the
picture of her standing at the street corner to solicit—quite
possibly a figment of his frustrated desire—he touches her
memory with one obscene word. Even so, he leaves her
person inviolate, just as in earlier days, when he still shared
her with rivals, he could heap obscenities on them with
gusto, as I have said, but never on her. If he thus refuses to
make her body cheap in his verse, it is because she had never
been just a mistress to him, but the embodiment of his
aspiration, the focus of his life's generosity and idealism.

His mood of love affected also his general poetic idiom
and coloured his verse vocabulary. He hails Sirmio as 'the
lovely' (*venusta*). Puzzled scholarship notes that 'the epithet
falls short, at least to the modern eye, of the actual beauty of
Sirmio, with its high cliffs descending into the transparently
blue water . . . ' etc.[65] Catullus was not thinking of the scenery; the epithet is entirely subjective; Sirmio to him at the
moment is his mistress.[66] He alone of Latin poets thought of
applying *venustus* to scenery—'the charm that Venus has'.
He applies it also to poetry, to modes of behaviour, and to
men and women, again revealing in this usage how these
different objects of his enthusiasm enjoyed a common content in his mind. Venus and her *venustas* move through his
pages and illuminate them. I do not think it is building too
much on a word to reflect that in the brief brilliant society
in which he moved, the charmed circle in which women
passed easily through the world of literature and politics, the
true lover's virtue became perforce the hall-mark of all virtue. Once a few upper-class women ceased to be chattel-
property, men were not only able to woo them, the best men
were compelled to woo them, by brain as well as by body, by
conversation as well as by kisses.[67] So the man who could

make love properly became the brief and exclusive type of
the perfect man, and the grace of Venus rested for a while on
that brilliant and fashionable group. Love's charm became
the general charm; her generous virtue became the test of all
virtue. 'O weep', says the poet, appealing to the tender-
hearted as the sparrow dies, 'Weep, Loves, weep, Cupids,
weep, all ye that have love's grace upon you.' (page 20).
Or again, a fellow-poet and friend is in the throes of composition, and for his romantic theme has already composed 'a
most lovely beginning'. And again, Lesbia has vowed a vow,
a clever witty naughty vow—and a 'lovely one' too. Or
again, when an acquaintance purloined that table-linen of
his, it was not only a 'sordid trick', but also 'unlovely'.[68]

Thus it was that the enthusiasm of the lover, the skilful
charm of the poet, and the witty grace of fashion blended into one composite character, that *homo venustus* which was
such a large part of the Catullan ideal. Even if none of what
we specifically term his 'love-verses' had survived, what
remained would be sufficient to tell us that this poet believed
in love, and seeing the world judged it through lover's eyes.
But this very virtue of his limits his audience. It gives his
verse just a little too much emotional enthusiasm for the
adult and middle-aged to read it with undisturbed satisfaction. A good deal of humbug is spoken about the universal
appeal of the heart. The power of love-poetry is very special,
and has to penetrate a shell of sophistication with which
civilized people find it convenient to protect themselves,
until the sophistication becomes a part of their own natures.
Having thus accumulated half-unconscious resistance to
erotic verse, they prefer to leave it alone lest it might produce a slight discomfort in them when they read it. The
young, whose emotions are more naïve and direct, are more
easily penetrated. So Catullus, who himself died young, can
be allowed to remain the property of impressionable youth.

WRITING to a friend who had asked to see some of his
poems, the poet once replied that he felt too miserable
to write anything at all; he had lost the muses' company, or as
he puts it: 'Sorrow has separated me from the scholar maids.'
On another occasion, complimenting a lady on her literary
taste, he addressed her as 'a better scholar than the Sapphic
muse'.[69] These two phrases serve to illustrate a problem of
poetic interpretation. How explain the curious paradox
which makes a lyric poet describe his muse as 'scholarly,'
as though he felt his lyric inspiration was derived from the
study and the dictionary rather than from his direct emotions? He remained 'the scholar' in the eyes of his successors,
Tibullus, Ovid, Martial. And yet, to a modern reader, his
learning is surely the least of his virtues. The riddle has been
answered by two explanations. One would refer his reputation for learning to the amount of so-called 'Alexandrianism'
in him, by which is meant a deliberate imitation of the
learned style which infected Hellenistic poets from the
fourth century onwards, and was a by-product of the re-
search methods of the Alexandrian library. This explanation
would force us to believe that his successors chose to
remember him chiefly by a minor portion of his work, a few
long and experimental poems of inferior quality, for his
powerful and significant verse is not weighted at all conspicu-
ously with Hellenistic mythology and allusion; he is in fact
much less 'learned' in this sense than many of his successors.
Another explanation alleges that since he was the most distinguished representative of a school of poets who set the
new fashion of copying Greek precision in matters of metre

and subject—a fashion which all Roman poetry thereafter
followed—he gained the reputation of a pioneer, and his
Greek learning was thus remembered even when later poets
had surpassed it. There is much force in this explanation,
reminding us as it does that Roman poetry from his day onwards was composed in the knowledge of a foreign language, and professedly on the literary models of that language. A Roman had to learn something of Greek in order
to write acceptable Latin poetry, and the modern world can
only marvel that poetry undertaken in this mood proved as
successful as it did.

But to explain the place of scholarship in Latin poetry
something more is needed. Any text-book can in a footnote
state the 'facts' behind some allusion to history or mythology. But the more we master this apparatus of learning, the
less sensitive we seem to become to any poetic meaning it
may have possessed. The modern indeed finds himself
dropping insensibly into the assumption that these things
are of themselves not relevant to Latin poetry as such, but a
burden which such great poets as Catullus, Horace or Virgil
chose to assume because they liked learning for its own sake.
It would be absurd in this slim essay to measure the poetic
success and failure of this learning in Latin poetry as a whole.
But at least it is possible to justify within narrower limits the
link between learning and that particular lyric emotion
which distinguishes Catullan verse. The two seem so incongruous that we assume that a genius of his particular stamp
must have taken a little time off for erudition as a sort of
hobby. But Catullus surely felt the connection to be closer
than that, or he would scarcely have described his muse as
he did.

If English were ever to become a dead language, a student
of our civilization might one day come upon a verse like
this:

They say the Lion and the Lizard keep
The courts where Jamshyd gloried and drank deep,
And Bahram, that great hunter—the Wild Ass
Stamps o'er his head, but cannot break his sleep.

On reading this, if he were a scholar he would be gratified to search Persian history for the proper authorities, if they exist, and show in argument how they were used in turn by Omar the Persian and Fitzgerald his English adapter; similarly is Greek mythology used by Greek poets and adapted by Roman poets. But if the reader were looking for emotional rather than intellectual satisfaction, if, that is, he were reading the lines as poetry and not as a linguistic exercise, he might feel disappointment when he read them over, sighing over the burden of foreign allusion which seems to weigh a little on the English verse. In neither case would he be aware that the contemporary reader of Fitzgerald might find an allusive quality in the lines, and derive a poetic satisfaction from the proper names, without knowing most of the historical data behind them.

I quote this example to illustrate the elementary fact that allusions to history or geography, used as a means of emotional communication between poet and reader, may become an actual obstacle to communication when they have to be translated. Catullus can write something which translates as follows: 'You ask me how many kisses I want? as many as the sands of Libya, that lie about Cyrene where the silphium grows, between Jove's sultry shrine and ancient Battus' venerated tomb.' (cf. page 16). Except for Jove, none of these proper names is touched with any emotional association for the modern reader, and one of them, Battus, sounds flat and positively ugly. But can we be sure that they were equally lifeless in the Roman ear? *Libya* might vaguely suggest associations of Carthage and Hannibal and past glories, as 'Spain' and the 'Great Armada' still do for us.

Silphium was a famed export of Cyrene, and a foreign and valuable herb which had become a proverb for preciousness. So might we name over a phrase like 'the Spice Islands,' and think of trading ships and distant suns and things exotic and rare. *Jupiter Ammon's* shrine, again, standing primaeval in the desert, was in those days of superstition a far more famous and romantic spot than any great cathedral site today. As for *Battus*, he was Cyrene's celebrated founder, and had sailed thither from Greece as the French explorers left France to found Quebec and Montreal. His tomb stood amid city streets, which were filled with memories of some ancient and famous names, Eratosthenes, Callimachus, whom Catullus himself elsewhere styles 'Battus' son', a symbol in his own person of all the brilliance of Alexandria. We do not complain if our own poets in similar vein name the names of Italian cities and men of the renaissance, like Florence, Pisa, the Medici, or Leonardo. Such associations are for us still living, but a parallel reference, which conveyed romance to the Romans, requires a dictionary of antiquities for us.

Poetry when it makes romantic use in this way of history, legend or place-names is simply extending the range of the image-associations which it is always manipulating. Besides the ordinary power of common words and phrases, there lies to hand a special area of reference, consisting of that particular set of proper names and historical incidents which may have emotional meaning for the poet's own day, and what these are is determined by the education which his readers receive in childhood, and the intellectual and emotional climate in which they grow up—the *ethos* of the civilization in which they live. Who shall attempt to tabulate all the causes which have contributed to the total effect upon us of a phrase like 'the Spice Islands'? Something clearly depends on the pleasurableness of the mere sounds, something more on their associations. These latter need not be very precise. Few of those who enjoy the refrain of 'We'll take the golden road to Samarkand' could annotate the historical and geographic reference. On the other hand,

> The mountains look on Marathon
> And Marathon looks on the sea

paints a picture in our minds distinct and definite. The magic of sound and association together combine in a sonorous verse of Hardy's:

> Sophocles, Plato, Socrates,
>> Gentlemen,
> Pythagoras, Thucydides,
> Herodotus and Homer—yea,
> Clement, Augustin, Origen,
> Burnt Brightlier towards their setting day,
>> Gentlemen.

Such a verse could never read as it does without that modern European education which gives us these names in the school-room. An American might not find it as easy to savour this particular verse as an Englishman could. But the area of association is usually wider, as in

> Quinquireme of Nineveh from distant Ophir
> Rowing home to haven in sunny Palestine
>> With a cargo of ivory
>> And apes and peacocks,
> Sandalwood, cedarwood and sweet white wine.

The response to such a verse is simple and immediate, because of its geographic romance, of place-names and materials. But not every kind of geography will serve. Neither the place nor the materials would sound so effective without their hidden echo of the English Bible, of Solomon's temple and the Queen of Sheba.

Latin poetry would repel modern taste less if we could remember that its authors were the first to try to make romantic use of foreign associations on a large scale. As pioneers in the art, they were often clumsy, choosing for their purposes inappropriate references and working the device to death. They were handicapped too by the rather narrow limits of that area of history which could have any emotional meaning to them. Troy, Greek legend, and some memories of Egypt, the Orient, and Old Italy exhausted the available material in past history; this they sought to extend by drawing on contemporary events, the Parthians, Cleopatra, Carthage, Gaul (to give a random list). Though largely unconscious[70] of what they were doing, they were expressing in literature the strong Roman sense of historical continuity, part of their genius for creating institutions which could last on—just because they were founded in knowledge of the past.

In literature their surrender to the past—typified in their obedience to Greek models and even metres—was too violent to breed an altogether healthy form of expression, and we need not enjoy all their attempts to recreate the past in their poetry. But we do need to realize that even when the historical reference is emotionally successful, we are likely to miss it, simply because the areas of history or legend or geography which had emotional meaning for (say) the reader of Catullus have in most cases no meaning for us. We share with the Romans, it is true, a general feeling for Athens and Greece and vaguely the Orient, but emotionally speaking this does not extend to details, like Callimachus or Dodona or The Seven Against Thebes or Cybele. As for contemporary history, what modern can ever feel the emotion that the Roman felt at the sound of the Parthian or Dacian name? Faced with the need to render poetic feeling from one culture to another, we realize afresh that it is impossible.

We can however make ourselves as sensitive as possible to the presence of this romantic element in Latin poetry, and thus prepared, we may be able to understand the occasional presence of learning in a place where we might least expect to find it, in Catullus' lyrics. I have already cited a verse of his remarkable for the fact that it began on the note of passionate love and passed from that to history and mythology. Kisses are compared in number to the sands, 'that lie about Cyrene where the silphium grows, between Jove's sultry shrine and ancient Battus' venerated tomb'. The comparison reads frigidly, until we realize that the poet has tinged the emotion of love with another, which can be labelled, not very satisfactorily, as romantic. He does the same thing on a larger scale in his bitter farewell to Lesbia (page 66). The opening verses look like little more than a list of far countries which a Roman traveller like himself might visit if he chose. India, and the eastern wave booming on the shore—the wild tribes of the Russian steppes (the names he uses are *Hyrcani* and *Sacae*)—the 'exotic Arabians'—the Parthian, arrow in hand—the Nile sweeping down to the delta—the towering Alps just conquered by Caesar's legions, and Gaul and the Rhineland, and even the Atlantic and Britain repeating his mighty name—such are the associations which he chooses to summon up as he writes his last bitter message to his love. The list is interesting. 'Nile' is an example of a term which retains to this day its associations of two thousand years ago. 'Alps,' 'Rhine' and 'Britain' convey a certain effect, but not the one they had for the Roman reader of 54 B.C., who linked them at once with the great venture in empire-building which was then being described in Caesar's despatches to the Senate. As for 'Hyrcani,' 'Sacae,' 'Arabians,' (as a Roman conceived them) and 'Parthians', these are now only curiosities in the museum of historical labels. We have to tune our modern imagination very finely to feel the note of sombre and even terrible splendour, carried with the names of far-flung frontiers, which the poet has chosen to blend with his renunciation of Lesbia, and which at once rescues the poem from any flavour of personal pettiness.

Catullus possessed to a peculiar degree that instinct which is able to use history, legend and place-names to dignify some theme of purely personal emotion. He begins the elegy on his brother's death with the sonorous line

Multas per gentes et multa per aequora vectus

and from this shifts easily into the mood of personal loss

advenio has miseras frater ad inferias.

Thus in two lines he does essentially what in the farewell to Lesbia was accomplished in six stanzas. Again, in a mood of morbid self-analysis he could write

Otium, Catulle, tibi molestum est;
Otio exultas nimiumque gestis;
Otium reges prius et beatas
Perdidit urbes

Here the order reverses; the thought of his frustration suggests to him the tragic tale of 'gods dethroned and empires of the past'. Very possibly his feeling for such themes was quickened by his Asiatic journey; the spectacle of present and past glories in the cities and ruins of Asia may easily have met his mind at an impressionable stage. *Ad claras Asiae volemus urbes* he says in a verse which hails spring and his own imminent departure from Bithynia. In the *Old Yacht* again, he describes with feeling the vessel's journey past 'queenly Rhodes and grim Propontis' etc. These examples are all from the lyrics.[71] Of his more ambitious poems at least three,[72] it can be argued, owe a good deal to his contacts with history and archæology during that eastern journey.

In nothing does he more clearly show that he is the scholar-poet than in the name *Lesbia* which he chose for his Clodia. His love indeed was a more complex emotion than we usually realize. In a manner easier to feel than describe, his worship of a woman, his sense of poetry, and his sense of history somehow commingled, without making his love in the least bookish, or on the other hand his poetry sentimental. To us the name conveys nothing but a sound, fortunately not unpleasing. But what half-conscious associations did it carry for him? It was in the first place an adjective, 'Lesbian,' used as a proper name, bringing back the splendid past, when poets lived on Lesbos' island and made it the great seat of lyric inspiration in antiquity. Adjectives like 'The Venetian' or 'The Florentine' might be cited as rough parallels for us. And secondly, of those poets the chief had been a woman famous and brilliant, and her song had been of love itself. He thinks of Sappho, that supreme combination of feminine passion and feminine intelligence, and he thinks of Clodia, her vivid conversation, her verse-writing, her sure touch, her emancipation. He does not call her Sappho; that would be frigid and insincere.[73] She was not another Sappho. But the aura of Lesbos was round her head.[74]

There is a possible English analogy to be found in some famous lines of Poe. He addresses a lady whom he calls Helen. The name and her nature call up for him the bright romantic feeling that he had for the classical past—

> Helen, thy beauty is to me
> Like those Nicaean barks of yore
> That gently, o'er a perfumed sea,
> The weary way-worn traveller bore
>   To his own native shore.
>
> On desperate seas long wont to roam
> Thy hyacinth hair, thy classic grace,
> Thy naiad airs have brought me home
>   To the glory that was Greece,
>   And the grandeur that was Rome.

Is it too fanciful to suggest that Clodia, the 'lustrous goddess,' was a Helen to Catullus, bringing him home, shall we say, to Lesbos and Alexandria?

DOCTUS CATULLUS — THE MASTER OF FORM

THE Greek scholarship which Catullus and his contemporaries imported into Latin poetry not only seasoned their verse with historical romance, but helped them to create new conceptions of form. The group borrowed metrical art, even to the extent of actual rhythmic pattern, from Hellenism, and this in particular gave them their contemporary title of *poetae novi*—poets of literary revolution. Though poetic criticism continually reminds us that verse form is a matter of conscious technique, popular notions of a poet and his poetry are always liable to lapse into the Platonic explanation of him as a man inspired with a kind of divine madness, which is another way of saying that his work cannot be explained at all. Particularly is this true of the *lyric* poet, whose existence we are prone to conceive as independent of time and circumstances, a wind blowing where it listeth. The adjective *lyric* is not satisfactory, covering as it does a range of verse-writing impossible to delimit and very difficult to classify, but those who apply it to Catullus are thinking mainly of those short pieces of his described in a memorable sentence of Munro, one of the poet's most sensitive critics: 'With him the completed thought follows at once upon the emotion, and the consummate form and expression rush to embody this thought forever.' Or again, in the words of a well-known *Literary History of Rome:* 'His full strength . . . lies in a handful of short poems, wherein truth to the heart is unmistakable, because the poet has mastered the secret of giving utterance, at once simple and strong, to fervent passion.'[75]

All this emphasis on the artlessness of the best Catullan verse is very appropriate if it is meant to describe the effect which Catullus succeeds in producing on his readers. But we can forget that the effect is an illusion, so successful that it may deceive us into contrasting for example Horace's conscious art which conceals art with the careless spontaneity of his predecessor. A contrast there is, but it lies between the emotions themselves of the two poets, not essentially in the extent to which each poet went in reducing emotion to precise expression.

Catullan lyric, with its apparent directness, bareness, spontaneity, on examination turns out to be no exception to the law that what we call spontaneous emotion is powerful only when compressed into exact form, and that the elements of form are handed down from age to age and from culture to culture. Lurking at the back of all our minds is the feeling that somehow, somewhere, must exist in purity a poetic expression of simple feeling untrammelled by art or imitation. We recognize that rules of composition are inevitable for poets on the grand scale, like a Virgil or a Dante, or for specialists in polished expression like Horace or Ovid. We can easily recognize the same striving after form in much that Catullus wrote, and it is not his best work. But we like to reserve a special place for his finest lyrics, fancying that here is a handful of verse, which he just wrote because he felt like that, in a manner beyond analysis, because he and he alone had an isolated flair for such untutored but effective expression.

I have already shown that in effect even his emotions are not untutored, that on the contrary they have an urban complication, and have also acquired a romantic tinge from his knowledge of the past. If we now examine the form in which they were cast, we notice that in metre, for example, the foundation of all poetic form, so far from allowing his feelings to flow in rhythms of native invention, as the early Greek lyrists had probably done, he chose to follow **strict** precedent, and a foreign precedent at that.

The two love-poems which express his earliest adoration and his last bitter renunciation of Lesbia are frank imitations of a rhythm traditionally associated with Sappho. Not only so, but the content of the first of them is as much an actual rendering of a Sapphic poem, as my verses are of Catullus. The spectacle of a poet, admittedly more naïve and spontaneous in his emotions than any other Roman poet, driven to a form of translation in order to describe his early love, shows how overpowering can be the need of exact form to express strong feeling.

Then there are the verses written in the eleven-syllable and iambic metres. To these, the lightest of his lyric verses, the name 'lyric' is frequently but unfortunately restricted: at any rate, they can for formal purposes be classed together. Their apparently easy and casual rhythms are also copied from the Greek; though in use from the earliest times, they were cultivated particularly by the careful Greek versifiers of Alexandria, including some who were his contemporaries, and by them utilized to treat occasional and often trivial themes in exact form. They cease to be mannered exercises when Catullus takes hold of them, because into such precise and dainty moulds the poet poured emotions altogether too hot and extravagant for Hellenistic grammarians. But whether he pleads passionately for a kiss (page 14: eleven-syllables), or is tortured by divided despair (page 52: iambics), this does not alter the fact that the patterns he is using are traditional[76].

For the two Sapphic patterns he had gone back several centuries, and we can guess that his two Latin imitations would have a slightly archaic as well as foreign flavour. For the lighter lyrics he still went to foreigners, but to a contemporary tradition. In his so-called epigrams, that series of terse and rounded poems in elegiac metre into which he compressed both his love and his despair, he followed a Greek poetic form which it is impossible to date by any period, for it had lasted many centuries before he copied it, and was destined to last many more. None other of his verses so consistently illustrate the importance of tradition in his poetry. They are a monument to the fact that true originality is to be found not in new form, but in a powerful spirit; that in poetry as in other types of art new wine is ever poured into old bottles. I have used the traditional term 'epigram' to describe the group, though the word resembles the wider term 'lyric' in being used of a body of ancient poetry, the content of which it is difficult to define or classify. It has also the disadvantage of misleading the modern ear, which associates epigram with a form of expression certainly not lyrical and not necessarily poetic. However, to understand the Catullan epigrams, we have to grasp the historical fact that he copied a definite Greek poetic form, a precise rhythmic pattern of couplets, sometimes a single couplet, of dactylic hexameters alternating with so-called pentameters, and that his pattern, once established as what we can recognize as a literary genre by the Ionian Greeks of about the seventh century B.C., set a fashion which held without a break for eighteen hundred years, and indeed ran coterminous with Greek culture itself.

The pattern owed its origin to the early need of composing inscriptions for tombs, public monuments and votive offerings. In these the Greek genius found opportunity for that supreme economy of expression which was its constant delight, and produced such masterpieces as the familiar epitaph of Simonides on the Spartan dead at Thermopylae:

> O stranger, take the news to the citizens of Sparta
> That we obeyed their orders, and lie here dead.[77]

To the end of the Byzantine period, some element of this terse reserve remained an ineradicable virtue of the better Greek epigram. To it was added another, an effect of balance or antithesis, of correspondence or clash, at its worst a mere pun, at its best an ironic or tragic paradox of thought. In its simplest beginning, the thing can be seen in another of the earliest inscriptions, probably by Anacreon:

> Of brave Timocritus the gallant warrior
> This is the tomb.
> War sends the man of courage, not the coward,
> To meet his doom.[78]

In these two qualities, of terse reserve and balance of thought, the mould was fixed, and into these formal limits the Greek genius for eighteen hundred years, and with varying success, poured the emotions of love, despair, hope, resignation, irony and humour. The frivolous accident of time, through the influence of Martial, has selected only the irony and the humour as significant of what we call the epigram. We need not marvel at this arbitrary preference for a narrow structural form, which would seem to carry with it all the dangers of lifeless mannerism, and which yet retained its power to express such a register of human feeling for such a large span of human history. Modern literature provides a rough parallel in the sonnet, with its conventional metre and length, its rhyme scheme, and its frequent habit of rounding out the thought in the last two lines. Its enormous popularity in English, French, Italian, Spanish and German, as a vehicle of the most varied emotion, witnesses to that union of conventional form with intense feeling which seems almost inevitable in order to discipline the feeling and preserve its intensity in expression:—

> But thy eternal summer shall not fade
> Nor lose possession of that fair thou owest,
> Nor shall death brag thou wanderest in his shade
> While in eternal lines to time thou growest.
> So long as lips can read, and eyes can see,
> So long lives this, and this gives life to thee.

This sonnet ending could stand as a fitting memorial to the Greek epigram itself. The words would not so easily fulfil their magnificent promise and live on, without their careful rhyme, their steady rhythm, their assonance and antithesis, and their monumental ending. The truth is that, expressing a strong but very simple emotion, the poet has disciplined it with intellectual effort, and the two combined produce a slight effect of intoxication in us when we read.

There is something of the same heady wine in the epigrams of Catullus, and for the same reason. I could illustrate the thing I mean in its extreme form by saying that the poet can sometimes express his most poignant feeling in a pun. Two of his epigrams describe in memorable language the division that grew in his soul: he can neither continue to respect her, nor cease to love her. 'Passion has so undone my reason,' he cries, 'that I couldn't like you now, though you rose to heaven, nor stop loving you, though you sank to hell' (page 54). This is a bald and feeble paraphrase of four Latin lines. Their ironic and tragic force escapes us, even in the Latin, until we let the sounds of the word-endings sink into us, and then notice that the balance and antithesis in the epigram is not merely one of expression, but corresponds in every way to the tragic contrasts in his soul:

your frailty	*tua culpa* ⎱	balance of case and pro-
my devotion	*officio suo* ⎰	nouns, but not sym-
		metrical
created a saint	*si optima fias* (passive) ⎱	balance of
committing all sins	*omnia si facias* (active) ⎰	syntax and
		sound, with
powerless to like you	*nec bene velle queat*	reversed or-
or to stop loving	*nec desistere amare*	der to avoid
		symmetry.

Then he repeats the paradox, with some deliberate echoes of language, in an epigram of eight lines instead of four (page 56):

you used to say you knew me	*Dicebas quondam solum te nosse*
	Catullum
now I know you	*nunc te cognovi*
the more extravagantly I burn	*impensius uror*
the cheaper you become	*es vilior et levior*
such hurt to the lover	*amantem iniuria talis*
makes him love more	*cogit amare magis*
and like less	*sed bene velle minus*

Each epigram lacks enough of symmetry within itself to miss the mechanical, just as the two together form a pair, yet neither quite repeats the other. They are untranslatable for reasons which inhere in the nature of the Latin tongue, and the imitations in this book, which begin respectively

> The office of my heart is still to love
> When I would hate

and

> Once you would say to me 'Your heart has found me
> And yours alone'

attempt merely to transfer some of the poignancy, through measured rhythm and assonance, into English, without the brevity and all the bitterness that goes with it in the Latin.[79]

It is a mistake to deprecate the presence in a poet of mechanism of this sort, or to assume that when we discover it we convict the poet of a fault of pedantry. 'None of the best epigrams' says Mackail of the Greek Anthology, 'depend on having a point at all'.[80] This is an exaggeration. The Anthology it is true abounds in samples of verse where either the antithesis is purely verbal, without any thought or substance at all, or else the thought is trivial. The 'best ones' certainly do not depend on making points in this style. But verbal balance and assonance carried sometimes to extreme lengths remain vehicles of poetry, and not by any means the poetry of light occasions and thin feeling:

> Then can I grieve at grievances forgone
> And wearily from woe to woe tell o'er
> The long account of fore-bemoaned moan
> Which I new pay as if not paid before.

Such patterns of words, constructed both vertically and horizontally, when used to convey powerful emotion, are as intoxicating in Catullus as in Shakespeare.[81]

When Catullus was happier, his emotions were less complicated, and he could for example express his complete and single devotion in a four-line epigram which it is correspondingly easier to imitate:

> There never was a woman who could say
> > And say it true
> That she was loved of any, o my love,
> > As I love you.
> There never was a loyal promise given
> > Faithful and free
> As loyalty to you, because I love you,
> > Is given from me—

a version much assisted by the fact that the English word 'love' whether in poetry or in life will stand a good deal of repetition. In the Latin, the formula of exchange is even more precise, especially in the last two lines—

> *Nulla fides ullo fuit unquam in foedere tanta*
> *Quanta in amore tuo ex parte reperta mea est.*

The affection is as it were itemized—in amore tuo, ex parte mea—signed, sealed and delivered. But let no one assume that such legal language is prosaic—

> My true love hath my heart, and I have his,
> By just exchange one to the other given.
> I hold his dear, and mine he cannot miss;
> There never was a better bargain driven . . .

The so-called elegiac metre in which epigram was written

was also used from the earliest times for verse which, lacking the cross pattern and the concluding point, could lengthen out into some form of narrative or soliloquy. It then became what is technically termed 'elegy,' a form as old as the Greek epigram itself; the dividing line between the two genres is not always clear cut. One complete elegy often seems to have consisted, as in the work of Theognis, of little more than a series of epigrams strung together. However that may be, elegy was developed in Latin, particularly in the form of amatory soliloquy, by Tibullus, Propertius and Ovid. Catullus however can be claimed as its inventor in Latin, on the strength of two poems in this book which by their absence of cross pattern and concluding point mark the transition from epigram to elegy. Both in their different ways are laments, the one at his brother's grave, (page 34) the other at the grave of his dead hopes, the wreckage of his love for Lesbia (page 60), though this emotion is again complicated by that divided mood of his, which longs to throw off the obsession but cannot. In both these poems thoughts and emotions pass into each other continuously like a running stream, whereas in a true epigram the beginning has been planned with the end also in view.

A wider claim is commonly made for him, that he first converted the epigram into what we would call a lyric. The claim however is too generous. As an epitaph, the epigram was from the first adapted for the expression of strong emotion, since it is a narrow step from celebrating the virtues of the dead to expressing the emotions of the living, the one objective, the other intensely subjective. The Spartan epitaph earlier quoted is completely objective; no hint of grief or loss mars its severity. But here is an inscription of roughly the same period dug up at Athens:

> Here lies a dead boy, Cleoetes son of Menesaichmus.
> Behold his memorial and pity him, who was so beautiful
> and died.[82]

The emotional distance from this to the Catullan epigram *For Quintilia Dead* or to the elegy on his brother is not very great. The difference is one of degree, not of kind, and demonstrates that through the course of six centuries the epigram had learnt to put the pity into words, passionate words of protest against the brother's death, and phrases of calmer resignation for the friend's wife. But the words remain dignified even so, and celebrate death with an economy and reserve which remains far closer to the reserve of the sixth century inscription than to the modern temper—

> Then can Quintilia redeem great sorrow
> Of early grave,
> Able a greater happiness to borrow
> From your strong love.

As for love, Plato is credited with a couplet, probably composed by the end of the fifth century, which runs as follows:

Star of my life, to the stars your face is turned.
Would I were the heavens, looking back at you with ten thousand eyes![83]

The conceit is perfect, yet so direct and simple in its application that it leaves the emotion free; to look down on our beloved as the stars do puts no strain on our thought. By contrast, even the familiar

> Drink to me only with thine eyes
> And I will pledge with mine . . .[84]

is just artificial enough to require a slight intellectual effort from us before we can begin to understand and feel. But in Plato's verse the emotion is both simple and powerful; we read it, and discover a love-poem in two lines, and then travel three and a half centuries onwards to the Catullan epigram and read, for example, this:

> There never was a woman who could say
> And say it true,
> That she was loved of any, O my love,
> As I love you . . .

There is a difference, but again, as in the epitaphs, it is one of degree. Plato portrays the lover's adoration in an image; Catullus goes further and analyses the feeling a little. But both their hearts adore.

However, though in his emotional power Catullus is close to the golden age of Greek lyric, that period stretching roughly from Sappho to Plato, this is not a matter of imitation; emotions, unlike the forms in which they are expressed, cannot be imitated and still remain authentic. So far as mere form goes, it was the epigrammatists of the Hellenistic period, some of them his contemporaries, who seem to have influenced his own epigrammatic style, though in his epigrams their efforts are transmuted, as they are also in his eleven-syllables and limping iambics. Callimachus for example could write: 'To Ionis Callignotus swore, he'd never love another more than her, neither man nor maid. Yes, he swore, but true is the saying, that lovers' oaths are not meant to be heard in heaven . . .' etc.[85] We turn from this to Catullus and read (page 50):

> My Lady says None other would she marry
> But only me,
> Not Jove himself, a suitor though he tarry,
> Yea, even He.
> She says—but what a lady to her lover
> Softly may say—
> Write it upon the wind or in the river,
> That pass for aye.

The reminiscence is there—the balanced repetition 'She says . . . yes, she says . . .' and the complaint that lovers' promises mean nothing—but the words are now the words of a man himself in love. Or again, Catullus' contemporary Philodemus could write:

> My soul warns me to flee the desire of Heliodora:
> The tears and jealousies of old it knows full well.
> It talks to me, but flee I cannot, for it is without shame:
> It speaks its warning, but speaking it still loves her.[86]

The verse has a simple grace, a restraint, which most of the love epigrams of the Graeco-Roman period lack. But its divided mood is not that matter for tragedy which it becomes in

> I loathe her and I love her—'Can I show
> How both should be?'
> I loathe and love, and nothing else I know
> But agony.

The Greek could afford to regard emotion at a distance; even though Philodemus addressed his own soul, he was detached from it, and ironically amused by it. But the Catullan couplet speaks only of the poet's own intimate feeling.

It can perhaps be claimed for Catullus that he was unique among erotic poets in making the epigram a poem of personal tragedy. Even the most sombre of those in the great Greek collection have a touch of reflection or satire in them which lifts them above purely personal feeling. Love, happy or otherwise, was by tacit consent refused such completely serious and tragic treatment as would make it the centre of the human universe, the place that it occupies in Catullus' verse. Yet if tribute is due to any Greek poet for helping to inspire the expression of love in Catullus, that poet is probably the Philodemus whom I have just quoted, a Greek scholar and philosopher whose lectures the young Roman may easily have heard, if he heard any at all, for Philodemus was writing and lecturing in Italy—the Piso family became his patrons—during the same years that

Lesbia was loved. The epigrams that he wrote are only sampled in the anthologies of the period that have survived, and his other verse has not survived at all, so how much altogether the young Roman poet imitated him we cannot tell. But if he deserves to be rescued from poetic oblivion, it is not for any verbal borrowings from him that may be found in the poetry of Catullus, but because he alone of the Hellenistic versifiers anticipated some of the simplicity and sincerity of feeling which is the hallmark of Catullus' most powerful verse.

The Greek Anthology contains a mass of pretty epigrams, by such hands as Meleager's, written to and about love, between the fourth and first centuries before Christ. It would almost seem as though love was discovered as a theme for literature before its emotional possibilities had been exploited in life. Such poetry suggested to Catullus those charming Venuses and Cupids of his whom he musters to weep in chorus for a dead canary. Among the whole collection there are a very few which seem able to contain a more powerful sort of emotion, and those few are under Philodemus' name—

> Queen of Night, twy-horned, lover of night's long hours,
>   arise, O Moon and shine,
>   Shine quivering through the latticed window pane.
> Illuminate Callistion the golden. On lovers and their
>   deeds
>   Thine immortality need not grudge to look down.
> Thy blessing is on both her and me: O Moon, my heart
>   knows it;
>   For did not even thy soul once flame for love of Endy-
>   mion?[87]

There is something of the solemnity of a hymn about this invocation, which exalts passion between man and woman as it was exalted only once more in the literature of later antiquity, by the young gentleman of Verona.

SCHOLASTIC readers of my imitations of Catullus will often be tempted to exclaim 'What has become of the Latin?' The present fashion of scholarship demands as a rendering of ancient poetry something different from what I have attempted. A recent translator of Lucretius remarks in his introduction: 'Each generation has its own prejudices as to the amount of freedom or literalness that is permissible; and in aiming at scrupulous fidelity in word and phrase I am no doubt instinctively conforming to the literary spirit of my own age'.[88] If the versions in this book have refused to conform to this spirit, it has not been from convenience, but from convictions concerning the nature of poetry. As a text to illustrate these, let us take the opening lines composed by Catullus himself in imitation of Sappho's love poem:

> *Ille mi par esse deo videtur,*
> *Ille, si fas est, superare divos . . .*

On this critics have commented, rather fatuously, 'He has failed to translate Sappho', or rather, 'he has translated Sappho's first line, and added a second and repetitive line of his own'.[89] Catullus however knew better than to translate. He is using a reminiscence of Sappho in order to express his own overpowering feeling for Lesbia: the result naturally is a blend of Sappho's mood with his own, and a mixture of her idiom with his. His own mood is one of adoration: Sappho in the original does not adore. In the extravagance of his worship he puts Lesbia above the gods of Rome—yet dare he do this, without incurring their jealousy? so he does it with Roman solemnity—'si fas est'.

So much for the Latin version. The English imitator in his turn is confronted with the task of transferring Catullus' feeling into the idiom of a tongue far more alien to Latin than Latin was to Greek. He can analyse Catullus' thoughts in prose as I have done, but he cannot render them into poetry and produce the same immediate emotional effect. Our age and mood is not polytheistic and does not instinctively fear divine jealousy. Moreover, he cannot copy Catullus' mood any more than Catullus could copy Sappho's. He can only catch it through suggestion, and therefore, though it will correspond, it will not be identical, nor will its expression be identical. Adoration of a woman in English needs different language: the whole business about the gods recedes in importance; it is the image of her physical presence that fills the stage, so this has to come first and dominate the verse in order to be true to the modern mood of humanism. Thus the Latin lines become reversed:

Ille mi par esse deo videtur,	To sit where I can see your face
Ille, si fas est, superare divos,	And hear your laughter come
Qui sedens adversus identidem te	and go
Spectat et audit	Is greater bliss than all the gods
Dulce ridentem . . .	Can ever know

This double example of an English imitation of a Latin imitation of Greek will serve to illustrate the fact that poetry can never be communicated through translation. At the best all we can do is to reconstruct a reminiscence of it. It is useless to parrot the words of the original; the imitator must contribute valid feeling of his own to make his result valid, and this feeling will require contemporary idiom to be substituted for much in the original. His task in short is less to translate—translation being an exercise in verbal mathematics—than to express the emotions which the original has suggested to him.

The Muse herself is responsible for these limitations on his powers, for her speech is never direct and plain, but always symbolic. Her symbols convey meaning indirectly through suggestion, and the stuff of these is impermanent, altering from century to century. The little dedication which heads Part I can illustrate what I mean by a crude and obvious example. He offers his verse to the public in words which rendered literally become 'To whom am I to give my new dainty little book, just polished by the dry pumice stone?' Now, this translation is not in the least a rendering of the effect of *arida modo pumice expolitum*. The poet uses four words, it is true, which describe the process of book-manufacture in his day, but his purpose is not to describe it as such, but rather to suggest in this brief reference the images of neatness, daintiness and loving care, and thus to communicate the qualities of his own poetry. The words can do this because their reference, to a book-reading Roman, is a commonplace, needs no explanation, and therefore leaves the mind free and receptive to the emotional allusions conveyed. The effect depends on this effortlessness, the absence of any tendency to stress the mechanics of the process. But this is just what a literal rendering does. It fairly pokes the pumice stone at us, because the process is unfamiliar, and to read of it requires an effort of historical imagination. We think where we should only feel, and the effect is ruined.

This not very subtle example, reminding us as it does of the vast changes which have overtaken book-production, shows how the allusive methods of poetry knit it into the fabric of the times in which it is written so that it cannot be wrenched from them. The verse of Catullus is as little immune to this law as any other. 'O sparrow', he sings, 'my lady's darling plaything'. At least, that is the way the dictionary translates *passer*.[90] But the sparrow, that grubby little bird, belongs to the backyard, not to the boudoir. Lesbia's playmate was both tender, precious and pathetic. At another time the poet wistfully recalls how his love came to him by night 'not conducted by paternal hand, nor fragrant with perfume of Syria' (page 44). The literal version can read effectively because of its slight suggestion of the rich and exotic, but it is not what the poet really wrote.

He only meant that they had never been married in church while the organ played, never could be acknowledged in the world's sight as lovers, blessed by a ritual which was conventional. Later still, looking back on a love now betrayed and frustrated, but overcome by yearning, he says 'My feeling for you was that of a father for his sons and sons-in-law' (page 56). No passage could more vividly illustrate the essence and the problem of poetic image. These words, hopelessly frigid to us, when they were written gathered up all the associations of protective and disinterested affection. To have said 'as a father loves his daughters' would have been inadequate to the poet's conception, because within the Roman household the women were traditionally treated too much as property to be loved with a completely disinterested emotion.[91] On the other hand, the 'in-laws' are included because the Roman family was by tradition a household, and the *pater* was its head, a fact revealed by the very usage of *socer* and *gener*[92] as familiar terms for which English has only clumsy makeshifts. When Catullus wrote, while the Roman family remained a valid institution, its atmosphere was becoming much more that of a voluntary association, wherein the attitude of the head of the household towards his menfolk, when tempered by affection, could reveal just that quality of protective yearning, spontaneous and disinterested, which the poet feels for his Lesbia. He surveyed his household 'as a father pitieth his children'. The poetic symbol, drawn from that deposit of associations which surrounded the intimacies of Roman life, needs a sociological essay to explain it, but no essay can ever convey its instantaneous lyric effect.

For such images the modern imagination has to construct substitutes if it can; if it cannot, then at least the obtrusive mechanical parts of the original have to be eliminated, to let the emotion flow freely and without conscious effort. This brings me to notice a recurring necessity which faces the

imitator of Latin poetry. He has to practice economy of the
original material, or else lose the poetry altogether. The
reasons for this inhere in the nature of the Latin tongue, and
are best exposed by illustration, taken once more from the
same verse of Catullus' imitation of Sappho—

> *Ille mi par esse deo videtur,*
> *Ille, si fas est, superare divos,*
> *Qui sedens adversus identidem te*
> *Spectat et audit . . .*

If, as I have said, in the first two lines the imagery is partly
foreign to the modern imagination, in the next two the
emotional suggestions though apparently plain and matter-
of-fact are this time too packed to be transmitted properly
within the same compass. The placing of the compound
adversus between *sedens* and *identidem* has an effect something
like this: 'He sits opposite where he can see you—keeps
turning his face towards you—and so watches you and
listens'. That is to say, single Latin words are heavy and
pregnant enough to require a phrase to render them; they
are more 'active' and less 'flat' than English words, which is
the main reason for the familiar compression and terseness
of the Latin tongue.

Words could not behave so if they were not inflected—if
their endings did not carry a significance of their own, distinct from the body of them, so that each word as it were
rings twice. Take this example from the first of the two
sparrow poems (page 18):

> *Cui primum digitum dare adpetenti*
> *Et acris solet incitare morsus.*

These literally rendered produce the following 'To whom
reaching after it she loves to give her finger tip and from
whom she loves to entice sharp bites'; a grotesque effect,
certainly; not a particle of poetic suggestion remains—and

why? 'To whom' does not really render *cui;* the single Latin dative becomes clumsy when it needs a preposition. *Adpetenti* the poet can afford to relegate to a tantalizing place at the end of the line, because its ending automatically ranges it, for the Roman reader, with *cui. Digitum* again, the finger, is by its ending ranged with both *dare* and *adpetenti*, an effect English can reproduce only by inserting the fatal 'it'. By the time the next line comes, the dative *cui* now implies separation, for which English is forced to give another and even uglier prepositional phrase 'from whom'. In fact, each Latin word in these two lines can be shown to carry the equivalent of an English phrase; 'She holds out her fingertip—and you try to catch it—your pecks are keen—and how she loves to tempt them.' Twenty-three words are needed to replace the image-content of ten.

Nor do the powers of inflection stop here. Word-endings not only allow a higher compression of meaning while yet preserving agility and lightness; they can be used to arouse emotional feeling by their mere sounds:

> *Huc est mens deducta tua, mea Lesbia, culpa*
> *Atque ita se officio perdidit ipsa suo,*
> *Ut nec iam bene velle queat tibi, si optima fias,*
> *Nec desistere amare, omnia si facias* (page 54).

I have earlier discussed the structural merits of this epigram. All I need notice here is the pattern of the word-terminations—*tua, mea Lesbia, culpa, officio ipsa suo: si optima fias, omnia si facias*. These are neither quite emphatic enough to make complete rhymes, nor quite symmetrical enough to be mechanical (*optima*'s case and number do not correspond to those of *omnia*). There is just enough pattern in them to point the antithesis and heighten the feeling—and what is English to do about it? To render merely the meanings of the words would be flat and prosaic; to try and substitute the equivalent in alliteration and rhyme would be artificial and obtrusive, because these devices in English obtrude more than the Latin terminations. English can only attempt to imitate the total effect by constructing a different one, which will carry an equivalent emotional meaning. And in that case, who is to say what is the proper equivalent? All one can seek to transmit is one's own emotion received on reading the lines, and the form of this, however much it strives to copy the structure of the Latin, will in the last analysis be a subjective creation:

> The office of my heart is still to love
> When I would hate.
> Time and again your faithlessness I prove,
> Proven too late . . .

It is to be observed that none of these difficulties are linguistic in the narrow sense of the term, for they arise less out of accidence and syntax than out of the emotional suggestions that accidence and syntax are used to carry. It is not so much involved word-relations as compressed feeling that baffles the translator, which is of course the problem of poetry anyway. The famous poem on the *Old Yacht* (No. 4) can illustrate what I mean by contrast, for it happens to be a study 'in the flat', the nearest thing to plain narrative that Catullus wrote, empty of emotional strength and complexity. Hence the comparative ease with which it can be rendered, as it often has been—

> Stranger, the ship that here you see
> Swiftest of vessels claims to be,
> For she can make a beaten boat
> Of any racing craft afloat
> Whether by rowing she'd prevail
> Or scud beneath the snowy sail . . . etc.[93]

Renderings of ancient poetry which strive after accuracy always please the head rather than the heart, just because they try to get in too much. English idiom and metre is too slight to carry the weight without staggering, a fact demonstrated all the more strikingly when we try to render the light frivolous Catullus. We discover that Latin even in his hands remains heavy with meaning. To take an unusually happy example, which yet betrays failure, Calverley rendered the opening lines of the *Salute to Sirmio* as follows:

> Gem of all isles and isthmuses that lie,
> Fresh or salt water's children, in clear lake
> Or ampler ocean, with what joy do I
> Behold thee Sirmio. O am I awake . . . etc.

This version pursues the Latin diligently—but the cost is too great: the long appositional phrase 'fresh . . . children', the careful epithets 'clear' and 'ampler', make the verse formal where it should sing, and entirely miss the light fantasy of the 'almost-island' and the 'brothers Neptune' which poetically speaking are infinitely more important than the fact that lake and ocean have their appropriate epithets. Economy has to be practised somewhere to produce English verse which is light and swift, and Calverley's version is an object-lesson in what to put in and what to leave out.

There is of course another way out of the difficulty. The proposed version can incorporate all the suggestion of the original in English verse which is fit to bear the weight, but this verse will have to be anything up to twice the length. It will be noticed that the more powerful English versions of ancient poets tend inevitably to stretch beyond the length of the original, and particularly is this true of versions composed not by professional scholars but by poets. Byron's version of the address to Lesbia in Sapphics (*Ille mi par esse deo videtur* . . . etc.) is an excellent example:

> Equal to Jove that youth must be—
> Greater than Jove he seems to me—

Who, free from Jealousy's alarms,
Securely views thy matchless charms.
That cheek, which ever dimpling glows,
That mouth, from whence such music flows,
To him, alike, are always known,
Reserved for him, and him alone.
Ah! Lesbia, though 'tis death to me,
I cannot choose but look on thee;
But at the sight my senses fly;
I needs must gaze, but gazing die;
Whilst trembling with a thousand fears,
Parched to the throat my tongue adheres,
My pulse breathes quick, my breath heaves short,
My limbs deny their slight support,
Cold dews my pallid face o'erspread,
With deadly languor droops my head,
My ears with tingling echoes ring,
And life itself is on the wing;
My eyes refuse the cheering light,
Their orbs are veiled in starless night;
Such pangs my nature sinks beneath,
And feels a temporary death.

Poetic instinct has here correctly recognized that the emotional force of the Latin requires to be dissipated—I think that is the just word—at greater length in English. So also G. S. Davies' rendering of the second sparrow poem, by far the prettiest and most poetic version available in English—

Weep, weep, ye loves and cupids all
And ilka Man o' decent feelin':
My lassie's lost her wee, wee bird,
And that's a loss, ye'll ken, past healin'.

The lassie lo'ed him like her een:
The darlin' wee thing lo'ed the ither,
And knew and nestled to her breast.
As ony bairnie to her mither.

Her bosom was his dear dear haunt,
So dear, he cared nae lang to leave it;
He'd nae but gang his ain sma' jaunt,
And flutter piping back bereavit . . . etc.

Neat though this version is, the effect in English is discursive, where the Latin is quick and slight, and no translator need hope to avoid this defect altogether in his own attempts. The general question however of whether or not to lengthen the English in response to the emotional requirement of the Latin raises an issue of principle. Is one justified in altering the genre of a poem—for that is practically what such lengthening may amount to if adequate—in order to preserve its total 'meaning'? I have thought not. The time-length of a poem, that interval during which it can be read aloud, seems to me an intrinsic part of the form of all poetry. To extend for example the time-length of the *Ille mi par esse deo videtur* or the *Lugete, O Veneres Cupidinesque* is to do something quite fundamental to the original mould in which the Latin poet cast his feeling, and since it is the mould, and not essentially the emotion, which distinguishes one piece of poetry from another, the tampering seems to me to be an example of real distortion. Economy is left as the only way out.

When finally we confront the problems of metre, the barriers between Latin and 'our sweet English tongue', always high, become virtually impassable. The original rhythms cannot be copied, because the Latin poets chose to write in the quantitative modes of Greece, which means roughly that if we scan their poetry precisely, it reads in the

artificial manner in which we have to sing English verse
when it is set to music, prolonging the long syllables irres-
pective of the natural pronunciation of the words.

This very artificiality however of the quantitative rhythms
gives them a quality which the imitator cannot afford to
ignore. They are amazingly flexible in their effects. How
explain this paradox? One would have supposed that monotonous repetition of the same musical pattern would have
made for stiffness and rigidity. To this there are three
answers. First, most though not all of the metres used by the
Romans admitted of some variation within the same pattern,
the conspicuous example being the hexameter, which by
allowing the interchange of dactyls and spondees could vary
from line to line:

> *Sí quícquám mútís grátum áccéptúmve sepúlcris*
> *Cúm désíderió veterés renovámus amóres.*

But this does not explain the equal flexibility under Catullus'
hand of other metres which did not allow anything like an
equal license. We must therefore notice, in the second place,
that the divisions between the words, which naturally fall in
different places according to length and arrangement, impose a kind of counter-pattern upon the metre:

> *Nobis, cum semel occidit brevis lux,*
> *Nox est perpetua una dormienda*

These two consecutive lines form quite different patterns.
The first is chopped up between its words, and is cut off by
the final monosyllable, just as human life is cut off. The
second prolongs itself through the heavy words, one of
them elided, just as death is prolonged. And in the third
place, further variety was made possible through the fact
that the Latin words could not help retaining in the Roman
reader's mind their normal pronunciation, as he would use
them in conversation. Metre required him to read with the

stress on brev'is lux, but ordinary usage called for brévis lux.
Thus the one set of stresses continually fought against the
other, the rhythm of conversation modifying the ictus of the
metre, as happens occasionally in English, as in

> But lét your lóve éven with my lífe decáy
> Lést the wíse wórld should lóok into your móan
> And móck you wíth me áfter I' am góne.

In this example, the last line represents the 'normal,' as do
most of the others in the sonnet from which these are taken.
But in a line of Latin poetry, such 'normality', i.e. coincidence between the ictus of pronunciation and the beat of the
metre, was rarely possible, and indeed seems to have been
repugnant to Augustan taste;[94] this accounts among other
things for the Augustan requirement that the pentameter
should end in a dissyllable, thus bringing the accent of
pronunciation into perpetual conflict with the rhythm

> . . . *fráter áve atque vále* (as pronounced)
> . . . *fráter ave átque valé* (as scanned)

The conflict itself however had to obey certain rules which
the poet recognized by instinct and which are too subtle to
be analysed completely. In short, he had to strike a series of
compromises between the two rhythms, thus producing a
continually varying effect. If on the one hand he cannot have
them coincide, on the other he must not allow his words to
fall in such an order that their accents set up an independent metre of their own, for this would jar hopelessly with
the quantity, with an effect such as Catullus deliberately
produces, to achieve parody, in

> *illuc, unde malum pedem attulistis*[95]

where pronunciation sets up a rhythm of perfect trochees in
complete defiance of the eleven-syllable pattern. This
example incidentally shows that a metrical 'foot' to Catullus

must have meant exactly this compromise between formal metre and pronunciation that I have described; a 'bad foot' is not an actual slip in metre of the sort that a schoolboy might make, but a failure to combine metre with speech-ictus in a pleasing compromise.

The rhythmic flexibility produced by these causes allows a poet of Catullus' genius so to manipulate a given metre like the elegiac or the iambic as not merely to vary the rhythm of his lines but even to vary the pattern of whole poems and adapt his metre to mood. This may serve to explain why taste and instinct prompted me to render the iambics of the *Salute to Sirmio* and the *Miser Catulle* in different modes (pp. 9, 53) and why I have felt able to treat the dactylic metres of the epigrams with equal freedom. Where the mood of the epigram was passionate, sorrowful or bitter the weight of the first line of the couplet and the finality of the second seemed to me all-important, and I have tried to render the total effect by a sharp difference between the two—

> O'er many a sea, through many a tribe and nation,
> Brother, I come . . . (page 35).

But where the mood, and correspondingly the rhythm, were swift and gay or trivial, a different English rhythm has seemed appropriate, as

> They tell me Quintia's a beauty;
> It's true she's fair and straight and tall . . . (page 25).

or

> Ah my love her lips how pretty
> And how cruel! . . . (page 29).

As for the eleven-syllables, their lightness and speed can be imitated only by splitting each Latin line into two very short English lines, whose total syllables, it will usually be found, also equal eleven—

> My darling, let us live
> And love for ever . . .

The absence of rhyme in Latin is no reason for its absence in English versions. On the contrary, rhyme is needed to supply the place of much in the formal structure of the Latin verse which cannot be transmitted, not only the beat of the quantitative metres, but also those patterns of word-terminations which I have earlier illustrated from the epigrams. Rhyme, which emphasizes symmetry and pause, can at least assist in supplying some of these omissions. Rhyme indeed, by calling attention to symmetry in the endings of words, represents the instinctive effort of an uninflected tongue to gain some of the poetic advantages of inflection. Greek and Latin verses continually produce half-rhymes within each line and between lines; deliberately to place such assonances at the end of the line would have made both languages unbearably monotonous to read in verse, since the assonances within the lines are inevitable in any case; hence the absence of what we call rhyme in classical poetry, unless monotony is intended.

Such explanations however of my own versions do but rationalize, I fear, methods which instinct first adopted. Perhaps the conclusion of the whole matter is that poetry, viewed as a historical phenomenon, is impermanent; its images and very rhythms are too involved with patterns of emotion and thought which together composed the idiom of the age in which it was written. England has been able to enjoy a continuous civilization for several hundred years, so that it can still savour its Shakespeare direct; effort has to creep in slightly to make up the experience, but as yet we do not need much; the case grows different as soon as we pass backward a little to Chaucer. But civilisations that vanish altogether carry their poetry with them; it is read if at all by a diminishing few and for reasons different from those which originally inspired it, as we can see from the instance of the Romans themselves, who read Greek poetry eagerly, but from a point of view which its own authors would have had difficulty in recognizing.

We often speak of poetry as the universal language, which everyone understands, and which in some mysterious fashion becomes the vehicle of higher truth. The reverse is really the case. It is prose which by seeking to reduce emotional imagery to abstract and rational form becomes the universal language and the vehicle of approximate truth. Only, since its aim is to reduce the emotional content, it makes demands on the more rational part of our minds. Rhythmic expression evokes the primitive in us. It can therefore be a means of communication to thousands of people who have never learnt to think; its appeal in its own generation may well deserve the adjective universal; it can be sung in the theatre, the street and at the table, as our fathers sang hymns and as to-day we sing popular songs, music-hall melodies, and dance-tunes—the poetry these of the common people, the raw material of all poetic form. But it pays the penalty of this easy but temporary communication, for the rhythms, images and associations which cast this spell are riveted into the social structure, entangled in fleeting time, as is the Catullan language, that transitory poetic medium, once quick and vivid and unconsciously conceived, now only matter for a 'theme at school'. Plato was right when he refused metaphysical honours to poetry. It belongs to the flux, and apologists who try to explain away Plato's doctrine concerning poetic art merely seek to disguise this essential truth. If poetry teaches anything which is permanently valid, it does so by accident, because it may happen to deal with grave ideas which could be as clearly rendered in prose, as is the case with Hebrew poetry of the Bible.

Poetry's own claim remains however unchallenged—to give enjoyment in the leisured hour. That is its final function, and almost the only one. Scholarship, which has set a gulf between itself and poetry far greater than any that existed in Catullus' own day, is prone to treat ancient poetry as an intellectual discipline or as a vehicle of ideas. Catullus can provide little of either. His poetry is very pure and youthful. His gift is the charm of the transient moment, and my imitations were constructed under the spell of this charm. If they can communicate an hour of this pleasure to others, that can serve as their justification.

(i) The *Poetae Novi* and their Significance

THOUGH Catullus is best understood in detachment from the rest of the Latin poets, he is no isolated freak. His poetry occupies indeed a peculiar and ambiguous position, exercising a powerful influence on the young Virgil, remembered grudgingly by Horace but gratefully by the elegists, imitated by Martial, discussed by Quintilian—yet among these not one shows any signs of catching or understanding the direct inspiration of his lyrics. This fact reveals something of the fate of Latin poetry. Two things in the history of Latin literature it is difficult to understand. The first is its decline. Poetry had exhausted its vigour when Juvenal died, yet the imperial system still had several centuries to run out. To the glaring contrast between the political effectiveness of that system, and the paucity of imaginative literature produced within it, recorded history offers no parallel. The loss of political liberty can scarcely be the explanation, for the Caesars did not and could not exercise dictatorship over their peoples in the manner of a totalitarian state. Daily life and local politics over most of the empire's vast area were comparatively free, and society was certainly secure enough during long periods to support a leisured and, one would have thought, a creative class. But while these conditions produced culture and scholarly writing, they did not create literature. Failure revealed itself in the lack of emotional content put into forms which rapidly became mechanical.

The second thing difficult to comprehend is the significance of what is known as the Alexandrian movement in Roman literature, led by Catullus and his contemporaries. This is generally represented as in the main a false move in the direction of artificial sources, the mannered verse, elaborate epics and learned allusions of Hellenistic grammarians. We have seen how little of such pedantry there is in Catullus. Not only in him, but in the fragments of his contemporaries, and in the record of them preserved by the next generation, lingers a strong flavour of originality and emotional vigour and spontaneity. However artificial they sometimes allowed themselves to be, surely it is Horace who thirty years later seems to resent the daring of his predecessors, deploring in the *Satires*,[96] for example, the preference shown by Valerius Cato, once leader of the new movement, for the rough vigour of Lucilius, refusing anywhere to acknowledge his passionate contemporary Propertius, and exhorting the writers of Rome, in his *Ars Poetica*, to discipline emotions and trim them to suit the exact forms handed down from the past. Who in fact should stand convicted of formalism—the Alexandrians or some of the Augustans?

Each of these problems however—the curious status of the *poetae novi* and the later decline of Latin poetry—can be used to shed light on the other. There is I believe a connection between them, which can be appreciated only when the nature of the poetic revolution attempted by Catullus' school is appreciated also. The literary remains of that school, if we except Catullus, are as scanty as those of earlier Latin literature, and this, combined with the fact that we read the Latin writers as it were backwards, from the point of view of Horace and the Augustans, has obscured the entire perspective.[97] To correct it I am going to offer a reinterpretation of Roman literary history. But by the very nature of the evidence it must remain a controversial and tentative hypothesis.

First let us remind ourselves of what seems to be the relation between matter and form in poetry. The first is the fruit of the poet's emotions. Unless these are powerful and sincere, he cannot write powerful verse. If they are, then they have to find expression in image-language and in rhythm; they have to attain form. Here it seems to be a law of poetry that the elements of form should be borrowed from tradition. It is as though the poet refused to concern himself directly with intellectual construction, and merely looked around for the readiest medium in which to express his feeling. But to be completely successful his instincts must guide him to choose such forms as will least impede his feeling with artificial effort. These having been chosen will in the process of use undergo some transformation at his hands; he will produce variations which constitute his own claim to originality. If we may guess at the poet's psychological process, his manipulation of form may be compared to the motions of driving a car. These, complicated and severe in their discipline, are nevertheless in the complete car driver performed in his unconscious, leaving the conscious mind free to enjoy the scenery or emulate a rival's speed according to mental capacity. Such conscious activity corresponds to the play of feeling in the poet's mind, which summons from the unconscious an appropriate form of expression. If the relation is reversed, and the motions of driving or of poetic composition themselves remain conscious, they may be equally precise, but they will not be sustained as long, and the total process will lack verve and enjoyment.

With this rough analogy in mind, consider the course taken by the Roman poets. From the time when we first hear of them in the middle of the third century B.C., they are translating Greek epics and adapting Greek plays, turning from the attempt to use native rhythms like the rough Saturnian, ignoring the stress accent of Latin, seeking to import Greek quantitative methods into Roman poetry. As for Italian lyric, we do not hear of it at all. The songs and ballads and rough spontaneous verse in which early Italy had presumably expressed its feelings survived neither in their original form, nor—and this is more important—as an influence on the first literary poets. From its recorded origins Roman literature marks an artificial attempt to imitate foreign tradition. The comic dramatists with sound instinct used Greek models which were practically contemporary in their appeal;[98] the epic writers did not even do this, but sought to revive in Latin a Greek epic style which in the passage of time had already become slightly archaic even among the Greeks. The general result was that Roman poetry completely missed that kind of direct feeling, which distinguishes Homer and the Greek lyrists and dramatists. It could not sing, just at that stage in its development when it was proper for it to sing. Moreover, the attempt to wrest Greek forms and metres to the uses of the Latin tongue produced, in the compromise between native and foreign, a roughness and clumsiness which the new poets of the first century instinctively disliked.

Rapid economic expansion, by greatly enlarging the leisured class in Italy in the first century B.C., created the soil from which sprang the 'neoterics', the new school of Latin poetry. They like their predecessors borrowed their forms from foreign tradition, though not, as we shall see, precisely the same tradition. But before this debt is considered, the first thing to realize is that the mainspring of the movement was an emotional release, which produced at last in the Roman breast a direct spontaneous sort of personal feeling which poets desired to express in verse. Without this emotional inspiration, the movement becomes inexplicable. Why were its leaders nearly all from Cisalpine Gaul? The list is impressive: Valerius Cato, the theorist who guided the movement, and his devoted disciple Furius Bibaculus, both of whom lived long enough to cross swords with Horace and the Augustans after their own star had set; Alfenus Varus, Quintilius Varus, Cornelius Nepos, Publius Varro of Atax, perhaps Cinna, and of course Catullus himself, besides a few others mentioned in his own verses, such as Caecilius and 'Volusius.'[99] Calvus is the only prominent name among the neoterics which cannot be included in this list. Now, one might expect to find cultured learning and artificial mannerism overstressed at the capital, but scarcely in the provinces.

The movement however though emotionally powerful was not naïve; it did not spring from the soil. It came too late in the history of the race for that. It represented, as we can see from Catullus himself, the most distinguished but a not untypical member of the school, a marriage between spontaneity and sophistication. These poets were capable of direct emotion, but urbanized, inspired pre-eminently by personal relationships, as illustrated, for example, by the various fragments in which they celebrate and attack each other and by the recurring references to similar exchanges in Catullus' own verse. Especially they felt the urge to translate sex-interest into poetry, a fact witnessed not only by Catullus' verse, but by those epyllia composed by the school whose titles survive. There was the *Lydia* of Valerius Cato, which perhaps celebrated his own mistress, and the famous *Smyrna* of Cinna, a study of passion, incestuous, it is true, but still for poetic purposes romantic. Calvus wrote a poem on the loves of Io and Jupiter, and then, coming nearer home, an elegy on his own wife's death (cf. page 114), a landmark in Roman literature, which reveals the new and more romantic attitude now possible in marital relationships between men and women of the same class. Catullus (no. 35) also mentions the *Cybele* of his friend Caecilius in terms which suggest that it was a work tinged with erotic feeling. In all this there is a flavour of feminism and of introspection; Catullus himself had to offer defence, as we have seen, against the charge of *mollities*, a charge which was apparently directed against his lyrics (page 90 above). As for his longer studies, every one of them concerns itself, directly or indirectly, with erotic themes—the marriage of Peleus and Thetis, the betrayal of Ariadne, the loves of Ptolemy and Berenice, the self-mutilation of Attis. The emotional atmosphere of the period can be compared to that of an earlier one which in Greece produced Alcaeus and Sappho, a period equally leisured, sophisticated, and yet emotionally direct, a period when poetry dealt with personal and inner feeling, when poets exchanged verses and spoke often in the vocative.

And now we face the question which these new poets were forced to face for themselves. Where were they to look for the necessary forms in which to express these emotions— forms which, as I have said, are never invented overnight, but have to be borrowed and adapted from tradition. At once the fact confronts us that fate had denied them a native lyric tradition on which to build. It seems incredible. Catullus himself is a highly finished product requiring a literary ancestry, and yet, if we greet him as the first lyric voice of Rome, we must assume that his poetic ancestry was not Latin. Was the Latin tongue then so impoverished? Searching the record before him, we discern a few doubtful names like Aedituus, Licinus, Catulus, Matius and Laevius. These, on the strength of a few meagre fragments and notices, are presumed to have written short poems in the century preceding his birth, but the fragments reflect no native vigour, no soil and sun of Italy; rather they seem to be anticipating Catullus in the imitation of Hellenistic epigrams and light verse.[100] The story of Roman poetry in fact stands on its head; it had produced a sophisticated sort of drama patterned on Greek models before producing a single song. What native song-tradition Italy may once have fostered had now long perished through neglect. So, just as Plautus, Terence and Ennius had turned to Greek models to inspire their drama and epic, the *poetae novi* were now forced to turn to Greek sources even for lyric, and thence borrowed their metrical patterns of eleven-syllables, iambics, glyconics and elegiacs, as well as the older sapphics and asclepiads in which Catullus made his few experiments. Thence too they borrowed the literary genres of epigram epyllion and hymn. The common denominator of all such poetry was its subjecti-

vity and emotionalism, that personal feeling which trans-
formed even the old-fashioned epic form into 'little epics'.
On Catullus and his school was therefore laid a double
burden, of expressing feelings of affection, hate, joy or sorrow more direct and powerful than any Roman had cared to
express in poetry before, and yet also of achieving a literary
revolution in order to do this. In order to sing in Latin,
Catullus and his contemporaries had to read Greek first, and
if we fail to sympathize with their enormous task, that is because we judge them by the standards of their successors
rather than of their predecessors.

But finally, what tradition was it that these new poets
chose for their own inspiration? Deprived of a native source,
they did the next best thing and chose one which was foreign
but contemporary. The significance of this choice is completely obscured in modern histories. The instinct which led
these poets to Alexandria was essentially sound, because
Alexandrian literature was not an archæological curiosity,
it was not 'classical,' it was alive and exciting and contemporary; it belonged to the same world. If one is to express
vital emotion, the forms borrowed for it must somehow
have an emotional meaning which is contemporary. A
painter for example working in a foreign manner may create
a new native standard, remoulding the influence he has
caught. The actual foreign painters he imitated might be
second-rate men; but they would be expressing an idiom
which as we say is 'modern'. The past can provide 'higher',
more classical standards. But for present creative purposes
they are dead. A pre-Raphaelite movement will never succeed in conveying an archaic manner wholesale into a modern setting and make a success of it. Either the original
mould is abandoned, or the result has to remain artificial.

The occasional verse, epigrams and idylls of Alexandria
may all have been second-rate; they were Greek and foreign
anyway. But they were still alive, still being written, when

Catullus grew up. The Romans listened to the lectures of men who were writing these things, conversed in Greek with them at the table, felt the touch of contemporary enthusiasm for this or that poet—it had to be a Greek poet, for where was the native Roman poetry? So they joined cliques and praised or damned each other's work, reading Sappho and Sophocles a little, but thinking and writing and arguing in the prevailing mode of their teachers and their Greek friends, the foreigners they could still visit and admire. Though Callimachus was long dead, Philodemus for example was writing lovely verse in the tradition of Callimachus, and so were dozens more.

By contrast, the models provided by Homer, the Greek tragedians and the early Greek lyrists seemed to these new poets to be archaic, and I think that one of the reasons for this lay in the gradual shift in the pronunciation of Greek. By the time that the Alexandrian grammarians had to invent the accent marks to preserve the memory of the Greek pitch accent, we may guess that in common speech that pitch was already being extinguished. Instead of being sung like Chinese, the 'common Greek' in which for example the New Testament is written was being pronounced much more like any modern European tongue, with a stress accent. The rhythms however of hexameter, of the old Aeolic poets, and of Pindar were, we can assume, such as seemed natural and came readily to the ear only in a tongue which was sung in pitch. Once the pitch was dropped, iambic metres and metres close to iambic became necessary if emotion was not to be impeded by artificial structure. As I have earlier said of the eleven-syllables and iambic metres of Catullus, they managed to convey authentic lyric because they lent themselves to improvisation, which is as it were the necessary raw material of finished verse, supplied in the unconscious mind. But no poet of the Hellenistic period was able to improvise Sapphics, Alcaics or Asclepiads. This the instinct of the

Alexandrian school had already recognized.[101] It retained, it is true, the dactylic rhythms for epic and epigram and elegy, but even these made too severe a demand on the intellect of the poet. To sustain them in long poems without sacrificing emotional sincerity became increasingly difficult. This explains why only the short epigram retained emotional vitality, alongside the occasional lyrics, while epic, even when shortened to epyllion, could not lift itself above the level of mannered exercise; the metre itself had become too stilted: one cannot write sincerely in such artificial rhythm, unless one has the peculiar and indeed unique genius of a Virgil, who was content to let a line cost him a day's effort. In so far, therefore, as the *poetae novi* made the eleven-syllables and iambics their own they were being moved by a perfectly sound instinct to give the conversational accent of the Latin tongue its normal play in verse;[102] they were seeking to undo the original error whereby accentual scansion had been dismissed, as too primitive, in favour of Greek quantities. The dactylic rhythm offered a stiffer problem, though even here Catullus managed to make the rhythm of his epigrams eminently conversational, if judged by Augustan standards of elegy.[103] The fate however of these forms in Augustan hands we shall consider presently.

And apart altogether from metrical reasons, Hellenistic poetry gave the Romans a direct emotional contact with historical romance, for it brought the past down to the present, as the works of the earlier and greater poets, to whom the label 'classical' is often restricted, never could. We can summarize the situation by saying that however artificial were the products of the Alexandrian movement, it was not artificial for Romans to imitate them. An apt parallel is provided by the case of the Elizabethan poets. They too were children of a prosperous commercial age which increased the leisured class and also enlarged the historical horizon through commercial expansion. They too fertilized their native inspiration by resorting to foreign sources and models, and so produced a new poetry. But these had to be the contemporary sources of renaissance Italy, which, though they were founded on the classical authors, were intrinsically inferior to them, just as the Alexandrians had been inferior to their own predecessors. But they had a living meaning for the sixteenth century, could be discussed in London taverns and read not as 'classical' but as exciting contemporary stuff designed to amuse, not instruct, just remote enough to be romantic, and sophisticated enough to provide forms and models and a style which, it was felt, English poetry needed at that time. The result, in Spenser and Sidney and Raleigh and a dozen lyrists, not to mention Shakespeare himself, was that same combination of learning and lyric, historical and geographic romance, wit and epigram, foreign and exotic forms blended with personal emotion, which distinguished the work of the *poetae novi*.

There happens to be extant a couplet composed by Furius Bibaculus in honour of Valerius Cato, the critic who led this lyric movement to Alexandria and schooled or inspired Roman poets to imitate Hellenistic verse:

> *Cato grammaticus, Latina siren,*
> *Qui solus legit ac facit poetas—*

> Dear master, who alone dost make
> Bards of the lads who to thee throng,
> Take these poor verses for my sake,
> Thou siren of the Latin tongue.[104]

To those with a historical imagination, this testimony to the poetic leadership of a professor would seem, judged by any modern standards, to be at first sight incredible. But a little more imagination still may assist us to catch the note of emotional release in these lines, and to realize that here, in this praise of a scholar of Greek, a teacher of metre and form,

is the voice of Roman lyric, denied any native traditional
forms, thwarted in its expression, well-nigh strangled at its
birth, yet finding a sudden miraculous and artificial release
by resorting to Greek forms and trying to sing in them. It
was a second best, but it served to create a body of verse
which mirrored the emotions of a brief brilliant age. The
verses and epigrams of Cato and Bibaculus, of Catullus,
Calvus and Cinna, the little metrical romances so vividly
conceived, yet so carefully executed in Greek colours, were
forced hot-house plants, soon to die as such plants do, but
while they lived they dazzled with a special sort of brilliance
and charm; and after Cornelius Gallus in the next generation
had committed suicide, and Virgil had turned to the composition of official epic, the brilliance and the charm were
never recaptured.

Thus we have the lyrics of Catullus, emancipated by
Alexandrianism from the clumsiness and the ugliness of the
Latin tradition, breathing, instead of its crude and musty
atmosphere, a free air. The results are to be sampled in
*Vivamus, mea Lesbia, atque amemus; Miser Catulle, desinas
ineptire; Dicebas quondam solum te nosse Catullum;* and the
marriage hymn, not included in this book, composed for
Manlius and Vinia—

> *Collis o Heliconii*
> *Cultor, Uraniae genus,*
> *Qui rapis teneram ad virum*
> *Virginem, o Hymenaee Hymen,*
> *O Hymen Hymenaee . . .*

This vivid and charming poem is a kind of example displaying all the paradoxical qualities which distinguished the
school of *novi poetae* at their best. The metre is Greek, but its
conversational rhythm does not flag for two hundred and
thirty-five lines. The invocation to Hymen, the order of
themes, the conclusion are formally Greek, yet completely

fitted to the Roman marriage scene and to the poet's own spontaneous emotions. The Greek learning, the foreign history and geography, are there, but the allusions are light and swift and add romantic glamour to the native situation. The poem is closer to Shelley's lyrical mood than anything else that survives from antiquity.

To the next generation the neoterics thus left a three-fold legacy; of naïve emotional power, which found expression particularly in easy lyrical rhythms; of neat exact form, both of theme and metre; and a fondness for historical romance which issued in geographical and mythological allusion. The Augustans and their successors remembered the last two, and gradually forgot the first—as indeed modern scholarship has forgotten it[105]—and this is the secret of those twin puzzles, the ambiguous position of the 'neoterics' in the eyes of Roman posterity, and the slow decline of Latin poetry. Not that the emotional legacy was at once forgotten. The young Virgil responded to it readily, not only in his occasional pieces, but in the *Eclogues* and above all in the great episode of Orpheus and Eurydice which closes the *Fourth Georgic*. This tale of romantic regions under the sea, of passionate love and tragic separation, is too rarely recognized for what it is—an example of what the epyllion could become in Latin when handled with emotional sincerity and sure taste. Constructed on the sort of mechanical plan perfected by Callimachus, of a plot within a plot within a plot, in the manner of Catullus' *Peleus and Thetis* and *Epistle to Allius*, it yet manages to combine romantic mystery, prettiness, passion and pathos in a kind of literary tapestry. Virgil never spoke again of love and death with the same direct feeling, and his contemporary Cornelius Gallus, who shared this romantic mood, did not live long enough to leave his impression on Latin poetry. Propertius too represents the same traditions of subjective emotion, but spontaneity has already begun to abandon his slightly mannered verse. *Haec quoque lascivi cantarunt scripta Catulli*[106] he says of his own productions: the graceful acknowledgment does not undo the fact that he is taking up an attitude towards himself as a professional love-poet. Thus he betrays that historical manner of the Augustans, which made them too conscious of themselves and their literary rôle, but produced as its finest and most typical products the *Aeneid*, the *Odes* of Horace and the studies in history and mythology undertaken by Ovid. These were all written in the old rhythms of Greece, which however close they had once been to the rhythms of common speech, had now in Latin to be treated as severe literary exercises, and accordingly were pruned with Alexandrian meticulousness. Such formal modes demanded a formalized content, and the result was the *Aeneid*, carefully planned, painfully written, some of it splendid, but half of it dead; the *Odes* of Horace, imitations of the old Aeolic measures more exact than the original, with skittish eroticism or moral commonplace for content; the *Metamorphoses* and elegies of Ovid, fluent, elegant and unemotional, or else morbid.

Sheer form has scarcely been seen again practised to such exquisite degree, but poetry paid the price. Such of the emotional inheritance left from the neoteric creed as lingered on was unacknowledged for the most part, and by Horace definitely disparaged. It was not the emphasis on careful form that he could deplore in his immediate predecessors. What he instinctively feared and disliked in them was their enthusiasm, their extravagance, so often productive of mistakes and absurdities which his cautious mind could satirize, but nevertheless to be recognized by the more sympathetic as 'the real thing'. Thus it was that the poetic instincts of Valerius Cato, the surviving champion of the neoterics, supported Lucilius' vigour and verve against Horace's cautious style, and incurred Horace's hostility for it. Thus it was that Horace on the contrary strove in the *Ars Poetica* to excise the emotional purple patch from Latin literature. His condemnation of it if applied to particular cases might be technically correct, and yet his general emphasis was disastrous. 'If, as we read in Mimnermus', he says contemptuously in the *Epistles*, 'there is no pleasure without love and laughter, then try living on love and laughter'.[107] It is a safe guess that the emotionalism in Propertius repelled him, for he never mentions him. Meanwhile Furius Bibaculus and one or two more tried to continue for a time the previous tradition, writing lyrics and lampoons and championing Valerius Cato. Such productions may well have looked clumsy beside Horace's deft craftsmanship. But they had a germ of growth and progress in them if they had been developed by successors, and Horace's work had not. Hence he also gives in the *Ars Poetica* that disastrous advice, uncritically swallowed by modern literary historians, to stick to classical lyrical rhythms, those tested by antiquity, and use each for its appropriate material. Such advice reveals the enormous gulf between Horace and the true lyric temper, which, as we can see in Catullus, not only chose rhythms without regard to their antiquity, but twisted them to serve new and more serious moods. Horace followed his own advice only too well, turning his back on what seemed the frivolous occasional verse of his day, imposing his own standards[108] as the true standards of Latin lyric and thereby assisting in the gradual extinction of Latin poetry.

For Roman poetry unhappily continued to follow in the footsteps of the Augustans in every essential respect. Neglect of native lyric by the earliest writers had shorn it of Italian inspiration. In the neoteric school it had sought to find a substitute in a foreign but vital tradition. Then it gave it up and having in the Augustan period reverted to classicism remained stuck there. For some centuries poetry was now exalted—so it seemed—to the status of a cultured exercise in Greek classical quantities and forms. It produced one more powerful writer in Juvenal, but his secret is his rhetoric, essentially a prosaic gift.[109] Lyric emotion fumbled for expression in Statius, and did not find it. 'Culture' is fatal to authentic lyric, and occasional verse, like Hadrian's address to his soul, forms only an aberration in the dull record. Serious poetry never again dared to revive and develop the occasional style for serious purposes. Those that used it apologized for it, and without Catullus' irony. As a result, the empire suffered from a fatal class-distinction in literature, between the polite writing of the cultivated who knew Greek and the vulgar polyglot talk of the market-place, the ribald songs of soldiers, the crude verse of pantomime. If polite and vulgar had mated, lyric would have revived and all poetry been reinvigorated. As it was, poetry continued to languish, until, the power of polite Latin having disintegrated, a new beginning could be made, in ecclesiastical Latin scanned by the accent of common speech, and then in the vernaculars which produced the early songs and ballads of the romance tongues.

As spontaneous emotion abandoned poetry, disciplined and subdued by artificial form, cultured Romans themselves lost the power to understand that in their own poet Catullus, and in his school, a miracle had struggled to achieve itself— passion, humour, hate, straining to sing, and forcing scholarship to be their handmaid. Posterity remembered with gratitude only the scholarship, which it assiduously imitated. The recondite allusiveness of the neoterics, which marked where they failed, was the lasting influence they left on Latin poetry. In the pages of Quintilian, Rome's great professor and literary critic of the first century A.D., Catullus is cited seven times,[110] and never once as a lyrist. The omission conveys a judgment on the limitations of the Roman temper as severe as any that could be pronounced by modern taste.

Such is the story of Roman poetry. It has a fourfold moral. First, that Virgil and Horace, despite their individual greatness, led poetry up a blind alley; the forms they selected for it were incapable of further creative development; all that remained was repetition in a minor key. Only their very special genius, devoted to the special cause of reconstructing a culture shattered by civil war, could have moulded powerful verse out of such archaic forms as they chose to work in. The force of their example made spontaneity in Roman poetry for the future impossible; they took away liberty of emotion, and lyric consequently perished, but its loss meant the petrification of all poetry. Second, the neoterics, in submitting to the attraction of a contemporary tradition, showed sounder poetic instinct than the Augustans. But we should not claim more for them than this. The road they took, had it been followed, might have led further, but probably not far enough. Their own failure to find vital form for narrative poetry, seen for example in Catullus' *Peleus and Thetis*, indicates that the inspiration of Alexandria was too specialized and narrow to fertilize Roman poetry as a whole.[111] We should therefore go on to conclude, in the third place, that the Alexandrianism of the neoterics and the classicism of the Augustans were both desperate attempts to replace from foreign sources a native tradition long since destroyed; the result was only heroic failure. The fatal blow had been dealt Roman poetry in those obscure centuries when the native modes were dropped and Livius Andronicus thought it a fine thing to educate the masters of Tarentum by translating Homer wholesale. Fourth, and last, we do not see this story in perspective because we read Roman poetry upside down. We read the Augustans, take their own estimate of their efforts at face-value, model our taste on them, and so form our conception of what was proper and artistically inevitable for Latin poetry, forgetting that the very metres they perfected, so far from reflecting any native instincts in rhythm and form, were an artificial importation, so that for example, they could never conceivably be sung as their Greek models had been in their heyday. Measuring a poet like Catullus against such standards, we notice only a roughness here, a greater license there, and an emotional power which we ascribe to individual eccentricity. Here for example is a sentence from a recent critical essay on the poet, remarkable otherwise for its sympathetic treatment of his work: 'Catullus showed true instinct when he went back to Sappho for his poem on Lesbia; but he lost his great discovery apparently because he had in his youth grown so much more familiar with easier metres and found the Aeolian forms fettering his impatient utterance'.[112] This kind of judgment is the result of adopting Horace's notions of poetry, and of reading his odes as though they were the real thing. Important lyric is not disqualified by being written in 'easier metres', but rather the contrary. Modern critiques of contemporary poetry would never dream of adopting such pedantic formulas; only classical scholarship still obediently strives to model its taste on Augustan practice. But the gulf between scholarship and poetry is (alas!) now far greater than it was in Catullus' own day. Should we not very properly rebel if we were required to read Dryden and Pope as a prerequisite for mastering the Elizabethans?

(ii) Catullus and Horace

This review of Latin literature has had to cast a very wide net, and its conclusions will be recognized as contentious. Let me therefore close it by comparing more closely the lyric achievements of Catullus and Horace. It is a comparison which must occur to all who know something of Roman literature, for these two represent very nearly all there is of Roman lyric, and yet even within this restricted field they appear as opposed and even hostile forces.

Comparison soon makes it plain not only why Horace is the only other Roman lyrist, but why the claim must always remain doubtful. I have already suggested that Catullus' two

Sapphics, read beside his other lyrics, would wear in the eyes of his contemporaries a slightly archaic air, imitations of a great but dead tradition. The same would be true of his single plaintive but rather moving experiment in Asclepiads (no. 30) a rhythm Sappho had also used extensively. Three is not a very high total for these experiments, and we may guess that instinct warned him of the emotional limitations of the Aeolic rhythms. But Horace, about whom there was always a touch of the schoolmaster, deliberately set himself the historical task of studying the original lyrics of the Greek tradition, the Sapphics, Alcaics and Asclepiads, and of 'marrying them to Italian measures'. His proud boast of achievement stands justified; he accomplished a *tour de force*, composing three books of perfectly charming museum-pieces, laborious studies which were polished till the labour was hidden, in metres mathematically regular. His achievement was in a sense dead as soon as it was born, but it immediately became the perfect school-book for the Romans themselves.

Modern criticism has lately gone so far as to suggest that Horace, to assist his readers in following these compositions of his in artificial rhythms, incorporated a sort of metric guide in the collection by introducing his readers to each new metre through a careful translation of a Greek original, which could be recognized by the Hellenists and thus serve as a pattern of the metre of similar poems to follow.[113] This if true only underlines what he himself felt to be the extreme artificiality of his task.

Such an achievement was to prove of perennial value and charm, but it required a stamp of mind totally different from the Catullan temper. Only by the accident of following certain archaic metres is Horace a lyrist at all. His whole inspiration and outlook is the reverse of lyrical. This is no defect in him. Rather it is true that he brought to the task of verse-composition a special sort of literary tact, exactly the right instincts to achieve success. His odes are historical studies in form. But form needs some appropriate content, however slim. This Horace with careful taste could supply, in one of his three moods. He could deal in the less tragic symptoms of erotic emotion with ironic detachment; he could moralize gently over friendship, Epicureanism and the sober life. Or he could abandon the pretence of lyric altogether, and compose short heroic odes in celebration of national virtue. None of these emotions are powerful except in the imagination of professional commentators. Horace was not a powerful person. He is a master of phrase and form and of sententious wisdom, products of what I have called the historical attitude in the Augustans. For these he lives when Catullus finds survival harder.

Yet Catullus in his inspired moments can make Horace's careful art look insignificant. Take for example the very Sapphics in which Catullus bids bitter farewell to Lesbia (page 66). His use in this particular poem of historical and geographic romance—India, Parthia, the Nile, the Alps, etc.—seems to have left an impression on Horace, for twice in his odes he writes what looks like a reminiscence of it. The parallels are instructive, because, showing as they do the two poets working with the same sort of material, they expose the gulf between them. The first echo occurs in the *Integer vitae* ode: I quote enough of it in paraphrase to reveal the technique:

> To hearts from guilt set free, to lives lived purely,
> The strength of Moorish spear and flying dart,
> The poisoned arrow's deadliness, are surely
> > An empty art:

> Across the Caucasus though they should wander,
> Or where on Afric sands the breaker roars,
> Or where Hydaspes' fabled streams meander
> > By shadowy shores.

> For once when I, the woodland's call obeying,
> Forgot my cares, and sang my love instead,
> A wolf beyond my boundaries saw me straying
>   Helpless—and fled.
>
> Yet mightier far was he than all the races
> Of monsters that the Daunian woodlands hem,
> Or lions of Juba's land, in desert places
>   That mother them . . .

The two concluding stanzas invite anyone interested to place the poet either in the Arctic circle or at the equator; the discomforts of neither situation will prevent him from loving his Lalage :

> 'Still in my heart shall linger her sweet laughter
> And her sweet speech.'

Thus Horace too tries a little globe-trotting before coming to his amatory theme, underlining his attempt to manipulate historical romance in this way with the epithet in '*fabulosus Hydaspes*.' But his amatory theme, unlike Catullus', is too thin to stand being combined with the sweeping effects of the Hydaspes, Caucasus, and the rest of the apparatus, and the result is a poem of incongruities which has puzzled the tastes of critics ever since. It reads like a parody because Horace's emotions are not equal to his conception. [114] His second attempt to reproduce a similar effect is, however, happier, and I paraphrase it in full:

> Friend, if I go, you too will go with me
> To far Cadiz or wild north Spain, you say,
> Or that grim shore where the Moroccan wave
>   Clamours for aye.
>
> But I still turn to Tivoli. To come
> One day to that old town the Greeks built there,

And rest at last from war and wayfaring—
    Such is my prayer.

If fate forbids, I have another home
Where the dear waters of Galesus flow
And sheep in skins go clad, where Spartan kings
    Reigned long ago.

I love that laughing corner of the world:
The honey there—you cannot get as good
In Greece, and olives are the finest grown
    On native sod.

There summer lingers, and the winter days
Are long, and vale of Aulon, that dear name,
Grows grapes that have but little need to fear
    Falernum's fame.

Those happy heights are calling you and me.
There by my grave you'll linger at the end
With tribute for a poet, and a tear
    Shed for a friend.[115]

This charming poem succeeds, where the previous one failed, because the poet abandons the ambitious Catullan conception of geographic romance used as a setting for personal passion, and restricts himself to the contrast between distant scenes and some local associations of his own Italy—among which he characteristically includes food. On this lower emotional key he manages to maintain harmony throughout the poem.

A good deal of nonsense is often talked about the immortality of poetry. I have already said something of its impermanence, and pointed out that the more vivid the poet's emotions and their expression, the more they tend to rely on the idiom of his own age. Nothing reveals this more clearly than the respective fates of Horace's odes and Catullus' lyrics. The former are exclusively a work of the intellect, the latter were born from the heart. But it is the works of the intellect that live longest. Because Horace composed what even in his own generation were careful historical studies, they demanded from the first a mood of detachment in order to be written at all, and hence display qualities which have the same timeless appeal as mathematics. His work-order and cunning phrasing are mathematical, and intoxicate us intellectually by their skill, as the less obvious skill of Catullus' epigrams also intoxicates when it is perceived. But Horace does not make the mistake, from the point of view of survival, of writing in the quick idiom of the table and street; his vocabulary is never colloquial. Passing endearments, diminutives, and slang were totally unsuited to such formal composition as his. His sentiments again never depend wholly on personal occasions; they are always generalized. One cannot in any case express much personal feeling in a literary strait-jacket, however cunningly contrived.[116]

So the lesser poet with the bookish method wears better. He is the sort of poet who might fulfil the Platonic demand that poetry should embody something exact, some timeless and philosophical essence, or else be banished from Utopia. Having put together three books of odes, graven with a passionless skill, endowed with an abstract life more lasting than the quick breath of poetry, he could safely compose their grandiloquent epilogue, written this time not without emotion—the most sincere feeling of which he was capable, his hope of fame:

> My Monument abides
> My Task is ended.
> The royal pyramids
> Not so ascended,

> The brass wrought in the flame
> Sooner shall perish
> Than my immortal name
> That nations cherish.
>
> The rain's devouring blight
> Cannot deface it:
> The wind's unbridled might
> Cannot abase it.
> The centuries may deal
> Their mortal wages:
> My monument stands real
> To all the ages.
>
> Not all of me shall die.
> My greater portion
> Shall flee death, and defy
> His vain extortion.
> So shall the future time
> Crown my example,
> While the processions climb
> To Rome's high temple. . . .

His boast stands justified. Flawless poetic masonry has a survival value. Economy and precision, pattern and prettiness and dignity—they are all there in the *Odes;* only the emotion is absent. But Catullus is all emotion, fitted to the tight thin glove of contemporary fashion. For this he fascinated his own generation: *'nil praeter Calvum et doctus cantare Catullum'*[117]—the deft gibe is Horace's. Horace could never be sung around the dinner table. But by this also was Catullus entangled in fleeting time, a writer of *nugae,* sparingly honoured by posterity, and forgotten altogether for five hundred years. He knew himself, and his probable fate:

> So here's my book. I know
>   It isn't much—
> A bit of a thing—and yet
>   O may it stay,
> My lady Muse, awhile,
>   Though men decay?

The prayer was as far as he dared go. A poet of his temper is ill occupied with self-conscious ambitions for immortality. But occasionally we still notice and feel his love and hate and grief, preserved in the cunning shape of lyric and epigram. Ephemeral emotions these, when spent so extravagantly on mere persons, 'dear, dead women' and dead men. But we become aware at least of a heat which while it burnt was very hot, and feeling it, are perhaps grateful if for a moment it warms us.

NOTES TO PART II

THESE Notes, which reflect the limitations laid down in the preface, refer to the following works by the name of the author:

Robinson Ellis: *A Commentary on Catullus*, 2nd ed., 1889.
H. A. J. Munro: *Criticisms and Elucidations of Catullus*, 2nd ed., 1905.
Tenney Frank: *Catullus and Horace*, 1928.
A. L. Wheeler: *Catullus and the Traditions of Ancient Poetry*, 1934
F. A. Wright: *Three Roman Poets*, 1938.
J. Wight Duff: *A Literary History of Rome*, 2nd ed., 1910.

THE CANONS OF CATULLAN CRITICISM

[1] Christopher Hollis, *We Aren't So Dumb, sub. fin.*

[2] This figure is achieved by dividing poems in two where distinction seems necessary (2a from 2b, 14a from 14b, 58a from 58b, 68a from 68b, 78a from 78b) and omitting three spurious *Priapea* (traditionally nos. 18–20).

[3] See the prefatory note to Catullus' *Dedication* in Part I. No. 14b, which reads like a fragment of another dedication (*Si qui forte mearum ineptiarum*, etc.) supports the theory that Catullus issued more than one *libellus* himself; a collection of his verses was probably known as *Passer* in the early empire, which argues that it began with no. 2 (note 28). The present order reflects a mixture of artistry (the grouping of poems in 'threes') and mechanism; the former *may* have been the poet's own device applied to such poems as were issued in collected editions during his life-time, since it is consistent with the elegant devices practised by the *poetae novi*.

[4] See note 11.

[5] Such is the indication of 65. 15–16 *Sed tamen in tantis maeroribus, Ortale, mitto Haec expressa tibi carmina Battiadae.* The comparative closeness of the translation has been confirmed by the discovery of a part of the original Greek; cf. Wheeler pp. 113–114. Catullus himself describes the uninspired echnique necessary for such exercises, in no. 116 *Saepe tibi studioso animo venante requirens Carmina uti possem mittere Battiadae.* These poetic exercises are in a quite different category from his creative imitations like *Ille mi par;* on which see note 89, and the prefatory note to the poem in Part I.

[6] 65 was probably sent with the *Berenice* (66) to Hortensius, and 68a and 68b were both sent, it is conjectured, at different times to Manlius Torquatus. Both 65 and 68a plead, and with truth, that grief for his brother has extinguished poetic inspiration; 65, disjointed and suffering from an imperfect text, includes one pretty but incongruous simile (the apple dislodged); 68a has the elements of a formal plan, resembling the pyramidal structure of 68b, with his brother's death as centre-theme. It is notable for two passages of self-revelation (notes 22 and 31). These four plus the *Dialogue with a Door* are often classified as 'elegies', a rather misleading title, which refers mainly to length and metre and the desire of literary historians to discover ancestry for the Augustan elegy.

[7] Strictly speaking, as Wheeler points out (cap. vi), the poem is more than half-way towards the elegy, but the story-within-a-story was a device of the epyllion, and the elegy in this form could be regarded as a compromise between the epigram expanded (as it is in *World Without End* and *Journey's End*, Part I, pp. 34, 60) and the epyllion contracted.

[8] The poem jumps from the voyage of the Argo to the scene on Peleus' wedding-day; thence to the spectacle of Ariadne deserted on Crete (with some touches that recall the Lesbia poems); then some narrative proper, summarizing the story of Theseus (with apologies at line 116 for 'digressing' into narrative at all!); then Ariadne's lament and curse: then enough narrative to describe the curse's fulfilment; then the spectacle of Bacchus and train; then back to the wedding-guests and their gifts of flowers and shrubs (with a lovely but incongruous simile of sea ruffled at dawn; cf. the simile of the waterfall, equally lyrical and incongruous, in 68b, and the apple in 65); then the song of the Fates (in which the sacrifice of Polyxena and the bridal consummation are placed in tasteless conjunction); then, to conclude, some most un-Catullan reflections on the decline of the times (note 32).

[9] For further argument emphasizing the almost exclusively lyric powers of Catullus, cf. note 72. As an extreme example of the false emphasis to which scholarship is prone, cf. Wheeler, who devotes 98 pages to the nine longer poems, and 24 to all the lyrics combined; this however is bound to happen when the poet is interpreted in terms of literary history rather than of his own essential genius.

[10] As, for example, in the soliloquies (*Miser Catulle* and *Journey's End*), in which grief, anger, determination, despair can succeed each other without breaking the flow or altering the essential situation; cf. prefatory notes in Part I.

[11] As an example of what such division may lead to, Frank (p. 11) classifies the lively Priapean lampoon (no. 17) as belonging to an early unspoilt period, and the inferior *Dialogue With a Door* as late, since it is taken to represent the poet's 'later' attempts to imitate Alexandrian elegy. If his artistry bore any relation to his experience, surely the order should be reversed.

[12] To be found in Frank and Wright. The biographical method received its greatest impulse from the publication of Schwabe's *Quaestiones Catullianae* in 1862. Merrill's edition (1893) followed the prevailing fashion in assuming throughout that for every Lesbia poem a place and context should be found in the reconstructed story of the love-affair. Wheeler (cap. iv) is more cautious.

[13] Ellis, *proleg.* p. xxii, notes three such, mentioned by Suetonius; and there was Valerius Cato himself, an older contemporary of the poet.

[14] Cf. the prefatory note to the *Epistle to Allius*, in Part I. The first line is supposed to conceal the name *Mallius* (*me Allius*) i.q. *Manlius*. Thus this epistle would represent the composition which in 68a the poet at first says he cannot attempt. Frank (p. 46) also conjectures that *Afer* (Munro's emendation for the unintelligible *aufert* of line 117) represents Caelius Rufus, who, being at the time the poet's friend, had introduced him to Manlius.

[15] See prefatory note to *She That I Loved* in Part I.

[16] Cf. 43.6 *Ten provincia narrat esse bellam?* (Part I, p. 22). Ellis, however,

(note *ad loc.*) argued that this means not Gallia Cisalpina but the territories recently conquered by Caesar, whither Ameana may be presumed to have accompanied Mamurra.

[17] *Iul.* 73.

[18] Ellis on no. 107; Munro on 76.

[19] Ellis on no. 7.

PESSIMUS POETA

[20] 50.1–8.

[21] *Epist.* iv. 14. Pliny was rather self-conscious about these *versiculi* of his, and reverts to the subject again four times (v. 3, vii. 4 and 9, ix. 25); cf. note 24.

[22] 68a. 15–18 *Tempore quo primum vestis mihi tradita pura est, Iucundum cum aetas florida ver ageret, Multa satis lusi; non est dea nescia nostri Quae dulcem curis miscet amaritiem.*

[23] 16.12–13 *Vos quod milia multa basiorum Legistis, male me marem putastis?*

[24] A continuation of the previous quotation from Pliny (note 21); in v. 3, Pliny defends his authorship of light erotic verse by appealing to the precedent set by a long line of Roman statesmen, much as one might argue that there could be no harm in writing a novel if Mr. Disraeli had done it. The passage amusingly illustrates what I have later described as the supremacy of *gravitas* over all other virtues in the Roman soul.

[25] Cf. note 23.

[26] Ovid *Trist.* ii. 427, 354.

[27] *Eclog.* viii. 37–41.

[28] Latin has no label for 'lyric'. Laevius (cf. the essay on *Lyric and Liberty*) had borrowed from the Hellenistic poets the clumsy term *erotopaegnia*. Catullus uses *nugae, ineptiae, versiculi,* and the verb *ludo,* and Pliny, besides echoing these, adds not only terms like *poematia* but also *passerculi et columbuli,* from which it can be inferred, not only that Catullus' *libellus* went by the name of *Passer* (note 3), but also that his verses were accepted as a distinct type after their own kind. The absence of any label describing 'lyric' as a serious and significant art form, and the use of these frivolous terms, points to the absence also of any concept of such lyric. Catullus used these terms because there were no others, but they covered all his significant poetry.

[29] *Epist.* 114.4 *Quid ergo? non oratio eius aeque soluta est quam ipse discinctus?* 6 *spadones duo, magis tamen viri quam ipse.*

[30] No. 49. Editors divide over the question whether the verse is sincere or sarcastic; the truth surely lies between the two; cf. my remarks on irony below.

HOMO URBANUS

[31] 68a. 34–35 *Hoc fit quod Romae vivimus; illa domus, Illa mihi sedes, illic mea carpitur aetas.*

[32] The *Peleus and Thetis,* after noting, in imitation of Hesiod, that the gods no longer visit mankind, concludes with a piece of pessimistic moralizing on the decay of virtue and the confusion of the times, in a manner which recalls Lucretius or Virgil; its pessimism reads artificially when contrasted with his normal gusto and readiness to accept Roman life as he found it.

[33] Cf. in particular the description of Suffenus, 22.2 *Homo est venustus et dicax et urbanus* 12 *qui modo scurra Aut si quid hac re tritius videbatur*, where Munro aptly compares the Plautine use of *scurra*. Suffenus, that is, was a sophisticate, measured by the standards of the Catullan circle, provided he did not ruin the effect by writing verse.

[34] 22.10 *Suffenus unus caprimulgus aut fossor Rursus videtur* 14 *Idem infaceto est infacetior rure;* 36.19–20 *Pleni ruris et inficetiarum Annales Volusi, cacata charta.*

[35] vi. 3.17.

[36] 14.6–7 *Isti di mala multa dent clienti Qui tantum tibi misit impiorum.*

[37] *Orat.* ix. Frank (cap 6) offers the interesting suggestion that the same canons of style reflected in the 'Atticism' of Calvus have also influenced the lyrics of Catullus; the two men formed a literary partnership. This seems to be likely, provided we recognize that 'Atticism' meant not mere plainness of diction but an elegant and fastidious use of conversational idiom.

[38] 57.7 *uno in lecticulo erudituli ambo*—of Caesar and Mamurra, no doubt with a double implication in *erudituli.*

[39] Cf. Ellis on C.'s diction, proleg. pp. xxix ff.

HOMO VENUSTUS

[40] Nos. 84 and 39.

[41] No. 12.

[42] 10.3 *Scortillum, ut mihi tunc repente visum est, Non sane inlepidum neque invenustum;* 6.1 *delicias tuas Catullo, Ni sint inlepidae atque inelegantes, Velles dicere.*

[43] 6.16 *volo te ac tuos amores Ad caelum lepido vocare versu.*

[44] 13.5 *Et vino et sale et omnibus cachinnis.*

[45] 12.2 *in ioco atque vino;* 50.6 *per iocum atque vinum.*

[46] 14.2 *iucundissime Calve* (the practical joker); 50.16 *Hoc, iucunde, tibi poema feci;* 2.5 *cum desiderio meo nitenti Carum nescio quid libet iocari* (cf. the imitation of these lines in Part I); 68a. 16 *Iucundum cum aetas florida ver ageret.*

[47] No. 23 is a good example; on this Ellis placed a grave interpretation, countered by Munro. On the other hand, the attack on Caesar and Pompey, in 29, has a measured bitterness, derived partly from the deliberate coincidence of accent and ictus (cf. notes 94 and 102), which renders it a notable specimen of invective poetry.

[48] 50.7 *Atque illinc abii tuo lepore Incensus, Licini, facetiisque;* 12.8 *est enim leporum Disertus puer ac facetiarum;* 36.19 *Pleni ruris et inficetiarum Annales Volusi.*

[49] 6.14 *Ni tu quid facias ineptiarum* (cf. 8.1 *desinas ineptire*, where he deprecates even his own passion); 14b.1 *Si qui forte mearum ineptiarum Lectores eritis.* But in Martial, Pliny *et al., ineptiae*, used for *nugae*, has become a convention; the irony has gone out of it.

[50] 22.18–21.

[51] No. 44, especially lines 16–17 *Quare refectus maximas tibi grates Ago, meum quod non es ulta peccatum;* no. 10, especially line 16 *Ego, ut puellae Unum me facerem beatiorem . . .* and 34 *Per quam non licet esse neglegentem.*

[52] 44. 2–4 *Nam te esse Tiburtem autumant quibus non est Cordi Catullum laedere; at quibus cordi est Quovis Sabinum pignore esse contendunt.*

[53] 22.14; 36.19 (cf. note 34).

[54] *Apol.* 32 d.

[55] 79.

[56] 50.11–12 *Sed toto indomitus furore lecto Versarer cupiens videre lucem;* 9.9 *Iucundum os oculosque saviabor.*

[57] 10.1 *Varus me meus ad suos amores Visum duxerat* (the collocation of the pronouns is affectionate); 35.1 *Poetae tenero, meo sodali Velim Caecilio, papyre, dicas.*

[58] 30.1 *Alfene immemor atque unanimis false sodalibus;* Catullus liked the word *unanimus*, though it is otherwise rare in Latin poets (Merrill's edition *ad loc.*); 77.1–2 *Rufe mihi frustra ac nequiquam credite amice—Frustra? immo magno cum pretio atque malo.*

[59] 73.3–4 *nihil fecisse benigne; immo etiam taedet, taedet obestque magis* (cf. the *benefacta priora* of 76).

[60] 30.4 *Num facta impia fallacum hominum caelicolis placent?* 11 *Si tu oblitus es, at di meminerunt, meminit Fides;* 73.1–2 *Desine de quoquam quicquam bene velle mereri Aut aliquem fieri posse putare pium.*

[61] Nos. 65, 68a and 68b.

[62] *Am.* iii. 9. 62; cf. *Trist.* ii. 431 and *Prop.* ii. 25.4, 34.87.

[63] *Aen.* iv, 327–330.

[64] The Shakespeare of the *Sonnets* reveals a similar psychology: his devotion alike to poetry and to persons, and expression of love towards either sex in identical terms, and a preference for compressing such emotions into strict and traditional form, afford closer analogies to Catullus than do most of the parallels usually cited from English poetry.

[65] Ellis, *ad loc.*

[66] But in a purely emotional sense. The love which Pericles exhorts his hearers to feel for Athens (*Thuc.* ii. 43) is much more 'Platonic' in the strict sense of that word, i.e., an attitude of intellect and will.

[67] Feminine emancipation struggled against odds even in the republic, and succumbed under the Augustan regime, when it came into conflict with the official court attitude, which demanded old-fashioned morals and an increase in the birth-rate; the analogy here between Caesarism and Fascism is fairly close. This reaction thwarted progress without restoring virtue; it merely demoralized educated women by denying their energies an outlet. Thus Augustus treated the unhappy Julia as a piece of chattel-property in the interests of dynasty, and was suitably repaid by her disrepute. The authorities (e.g., Sallust on Sempronia, Cicero on Clodia, and, in the Empire, Seneca, Juvenal and Tacitus) are all on the side of virtue, and with masculine hypocrisy avoid confronting the real issue; scholarship has been content to repeat their diagnosis, cf. Munro's essay on *Lesbia*, and Wright, p. 128. Frank truly remarks of Plutarch that the only reasons which he could imagine for Clodia's visits to Cicero were amatory, so foreign to him seemed the notion of women in politics. Cleopatra was detested not more as a military threat than as the type of emancipated woman—*non humilis mulier.*

[68] 35. 17–18 *est enim venuste Magna Caecilio incohata Mater;* 36. 16–17 *Acceptum face redditumque votum Si non inlepidum neque invenustum est;* 12.5 *Quamvis sordida res et invenusta est.* Note also how his usage of *ludo* and *lusus* conveys the

senses of lyric verse, love verse, elegant amusement and sexual enjoyment; the exact shade of meaning shifts with the context: 2.9 *Tecum ludere sicut ipsa possem;* 50.2 *multum lusimus in meis tabellis;* 61.209–211 *vestri . . . Multa milia ludi. Ludite ut libet, et brevi Liberos date; ib.* 231–2 *Claudite ostia, virgines; Lusimus satis;* 68a.17 *Multa satis lusi.*

DOCTUS CATULLUS — THE ROMANTIC SCHOLAR

[69] 65.1–2 *cura . . . Sevocat a doctis, Ortale, virginibus;* 35.16–17 *Sapphica puella Musa doctior.*

[70] Verrall *Collected Studies*, p. 222 remarks of Longinus that 'he ignores the effect, the calculated and legitimate effect, of literary association'.

[71] The list can easily be extended: cf. in particular the sonorous succession of names, combining both historical and contemporary associations, in 36.12 ff. *Quae sanctum Idalium Uriosque apertos, Quaeque Ancona Cnidumque harundinosam Colis, quaeque Amathunta, quaeque Golgos, Quaeque Durrachium Hadriae tabernam;* this puts romance into even a playful poem, as, in the case of no. 11, it had been inserted into a tragic context. He himself indirectly describes this feeling of his for place-names and historical associations in 9.6 *audiamque Hiberum Narrantem loca, facta, nationes;* so in no 4 he makes the *phasellus* tell its own romantic tale of voyaging.

[72] The *Attis, Peleus and Thetis* and the *Epistle to Allius*. But nothing shows more clearly how essentially lyrical was his genius than the fact that he could manage this feeling for place-names and history-names far better in his lyrics than in his longer pieces, where one would think it more naturally belonged. The device was a gift of the *novi poetae* to Latin poetry (cf. the essay on *Lyric and Liberty*). Virgil's tale of Orpheus and Eurydice makes striking use of it.

[73] Or else playful, as when he calls Caecilius' sweetheart *Sapphica puella Musa doctior* (note 69).

[74] Scholarship has been curiously unimaginative in treating the name *Lesbia* as a mere literary accident; cf. Wright, p. 133 (where the argument is much the same as Munro's).

DOCTUS CATULLUS — THE MASTER OF FORM

[75] Munro in *Catullus and Horace;* Wight Duff, p. 322.

[76] The effect of tradition on his short verses (other than epigram) is difficult to estimate because of the almost total loss of Hellenistic lyric (other than epigram) (cf. note 101). It therefore receives correspondingly less treatment here, but I do not mean to imply that his eleven-syllables and iambics are any less artful than his epigrams; many of them deserve the label 'epigram' themselves, just as so many of the epigrams are lyrics.

[77] *Anth. Pal.* vii. 249.

[78] *Anth. Pal.* vii. 160.

[79] A similar analysis of structure in the epigram *For Quintilia Dead* will be found in the prefatory note to the poem in Part I.

[80] *Select Epigrams from the Greek Anthology*, introd. 1.

[81] Cf. note 64.

[82] *C.I.A.* 477 c, quoted by Mackail, section 3, no. 37.

[83] *Anth. Pal.* vii. 669.

[84] Jonson obtained the conceit *via* Philostratus from an epigram of Agathias, *Anth. Pal.* v. 261.

[85] Callim. *epig.* 26.

[86] *Anth. Pal.* v. 24.

[87] *Anth. Pal.* v. 123; cf. also *Anth. Pal.* vi. 349, by the same author (Mackail 2.6) which is a deliberate attempt to manipulate the romantic associations of proper names, starting with mythology and ending with the Peiraeus. It has been conjectured (Frank, p. 83) that the person attacked by Catullus as the 'little Socrates' (no. 47) may be Philodemus. If so, the attack had nothing to do with poetry.

THE IMPERMANENCE OF POETRY

[88] R. C. Trevelyan in the introduction to his translation of Lucretius.

[89] Wright (p. 133), viewing the poem merely as a translation, describes it as a 'predestined failure', and adds 'Catullus perhaps hardly realizes that the quality of Sappho's love for her friend is very different from that of his passion for Clodia.' But it is surely rash to assume that the poet lacked common intelligence. Such explanations reflect the unfortunate influence of that theory which would partition the poet into a young naïve Catullus and a more mature sophisticate which he later became (cf. note 11, on this partitioning, and note 74, on the name *Lesbia*).

[90] But cf. Butler, *Alps and Sanctuaries*, p. 230, on the *passero solitario*, an Italian song-bird (cited Wright, p. 133).

[91] Cicero's feeling for his daughter reflects the growth of a more 'civilized' attitude, but his was not the traditional ethos of Roman society in this matter.

[92] Hence the effectiveness of the attack on Caesar and Pompey as 'partners in crime' (note 47), ending with the pungent line *Socer generque perdidistis omnia.* This cannot be paraphrased, because its effect relies on the associations in the Roman mind which surrounded such a marriage-tie.

[93] G. S. Davies' version.

[94] Though apparently not to the taste of Catullus. This matter of word-accent is of some importance in judging his poetry and grasping its secret. He was able to write lyrically partly because he refused to let the Greek quantitative metres become a strait-jacket for his Latin; cf. my remarks on this in the next essay, and notes 47 and 102.

[95] 14.22; the parody was pointed out by Verrall in his article *A Metrical Jest of Catullus (Collected Studies*, p. 253 ff.) though I have simplified his account of it.

LYRIC AND LIBERTY

[96] *Sat.* 1, 4 and 10.

[97] A sentence from Wight Duff (p. 272) can serve to illustrate this distorted perspective, which has affected all the handbooks—'No literary movement had been more phenomenal than the Alexandrianism which fascinated the circle of Catullus and shrank before the more unfettered art of Virgil and Horace.' When confronted with the difficulty that, in contrast to the Augustans, Catullus is anything but 'fettered', reply is made that in so far as he was unfettered, he was not an Alexandrian, i.e., not really one of the *poetae novi;*

so criticism falls back on the theory of the 'two Catulluses', and supports one false hypothesis by another. The aim of the present essay is not to misrepresent the *poetae novi* as greater than they were, but to show that they at least represented a move in the right direction, and that the free 'unfettered' quality in Catullus' art derives in no small measure from his association with this movement.

⁹⁸ To be more precise, Plautus and Terence paraphrased Greek comic drama which was more than contemporary; it was more 'modern' and sophisticated than their rustic audiences. Wheeler, p. 72 well observes that the most popular play produced by each dramatist was also the coarsest—the *Casina* and the *Eunuchus*.

⁹⁹ In the next generation, Cornelius Gallus and Virgil, both Transpadanes, continue the romantic tradition.

¹⁰⁰ Cf. the interesting discussion in Wheeler, cap. 3. These names belong to the period of that influx of Greek letters into Italy, attested by Cicero's *Pro Archia*.

¹⁰¹ Since Hellenistic lyric (except epigram) has not survived, some mystery surrounds the story of the 'occasional metres'. The tradition tends to represent them as the special property of the Hellenistic period; the eleven-syllable, for example, was labelled *Phalaecian* after a late poet of uncertain date; yet it was obviously sung in Athens in the fifth century (cf. the *scolia*, including the familiar one celebrating Harmodius and Aristogeiton); the iambic again was nearly as old as Greek poetry, but particularly in its choliambic (limping) form, as manipulated by Theocritus, Callimachus and others (Ellis *proleg*. xlii), and as Romanized by Laevius *circa* 100 B.C., it is represented as an 'Alexandrian' metre. As for the Glyconic, which Sappho herself employed, its usage by Catullus in the *Marriage Song* is presumed (by Wilamowitz, cited Wheeler, p. 274, n. 64) to have been modelled on a specifically Hellenistic form of stanza. These (with the *Priapean*, Cat. no 17) comprise what I have called the 'conversational' rhythms, in which Catullus' lyric genius found pre-eminent expression. The truth seems to be that these like all others may have been as old as Greek poetry, but as long as the pitch accent prevailed they were used as it were casually, poetic instinct demanding for serious lyric emotion what now appear to be more elaborate rhythmic constructions; in the drama conversation dropped naturally into iambic, as against the complex patterns of the choral lyrics. With the change in pronunciation, Hellenistic poets came instinctively to recognize the 'easier' metres as more natural. But the poets' emotional capacities were feeble, so they continued to refine on the rhythms without giving them their proper lyric content, until Catullus took them and began to use them as they deserved.

¹⁰² Cf. notes 47, 94 and 103. In the only two pure iambic poems in the Catullan collecton, metrical ictus and word accent coincide throughout, which as Munro observed contributes greatly to their effectiveness. From these two extreme examples, which however do not in the least read like artificial exercises, it can be inferred that in general Catullus' instinct would recognize a poetic advantage, other things being equal, in metres which did not over-ride the word accent unduly, as the dactylic and Aeolian rhythms were bound to do.

¹⁰³ This can be discovered by reading aloud, e.g., the lament for his brother

or the *Dicebas quondam solum te nosse Catullum;* I have observed that beginners find such easier to scan, just because accent and metrical ictus tend to coincide. Munro well remarks (on no 64) 'We are used to learn our hendecasyllables from Catullus, our elegiacs from Ovid; therefore we look on Catullus' elegiacs as excessively harsh in rhythm and prosody; but do not feel his hendecasyllables to be so. This is the mere result of habit.' In saying this, however, he is not concerned with the coincidence of accent and ictus.

[104] I borrow this delightful paraphrase from Wright, p. 110.

[105] Wight Duff, p. 273—'It was by natural law that Virgil and Horace should recoil from the romanticism of the "neoterics".'

[106] Prop. ii. 34, 87.

[107] *Ep.* i. vi. 65, which Frank takes as a reference to Propertius.

[108] Frank (p. 269) argues that 'in the eyes of Horace Catullus had disregarded the proprieties, and Horace, who knew *the facts*, was correct in calling his predecessors to task for abusing their privileges and disregarding the obligation to give ear to fitness and to study *well-established conventions*' (my italics). But who except Horace himself was responsible for making these conventions 'well established' in Latin poetry? ,

[109] I mean no disparagement of Juvenal's powers, but only that they are of a peculiar order, and belong to a very special and limited area of poetry. The rhetorical poet has to be judged by laws all his own; there will always be those, for example, who will deny that Samuel Johnson was a poet at all.

[110] Quint. i.5.8 and 20; vi.3.18; ix.3.16; ix.4.141; x.1.96; xi.1.38.

[111] It is arguable, however, that such experiments as the *Old Yacht* (pure iambics) and the *Miser Catulle* (limping iambics) could have pointed the way to new forms of sustained narrative and reflective poetry respectively, if the Augustans had not deliberately preferred for these purposes to imitate hexameter and elegy; cf. the prefatory note to *Miser Catulle* in Part I.

[112] Frank, p. 107.

[113] Frank, pp. 234-238. This suggestion of Horace's purpose, though not this method of achieving it, was anticipated by Verrall's essay on the *Latin Sapphic* (*Collected Studies*, pp. 236ff), where V. argues that because Sapphics and Alcaics would sound foreign to a Roman ear, Horace wrote them in such a way that by following the word accent, and not the quantity, they could be scanned in alternative and familiar rhythms, e.g. *Sáepius véntis ágitatur íngens Pínus et célsae gráviore cásu* etc. He goes on to argue that, as might be expected, the attempt to acclimatise Aeolic rhythms to Latin was a failure. The sapphics of Statius are 'stiff, formal, lifeless, foreign, unnatural'.

[114] Munro (essay on *Catullus and Horace*) also dissects this ode at Horace's expense, but concentrates his attack on the last two stanzas, which he infers Horace imitated from the *Acme and Septimius*.

[115] *Odes* ii.6.

[116] By 'strait-jacket' I mean poetic forms which are not simply strict—Catullan epigram and English sonnet have earlier been cited as examples of strict form—but also artificial to the ear of the reader. Contrast the strictness of Tennyson's normal prosody with the 'artificiality' of his attempts in classical metres.

[117] *Sat.* i.x.19; *doctus* is probably meant as a sneer at the one Latin poet who had managed to win the title of 'scholar'.

INDEX